Why Kids Struggle In School:

A Guide to Overcoming Underachievement

Why Kids Struggle In School:

A Guide to
Overcoming Underachievement

Jerry Wilde, Ph. D.

Northwest Publishing, Inc.
Salt Lake City, Utah

Why Kids Struggle in School

For information address: Northwest Publishing, Inc.
6906 South 300 West, Salt Lake City, Utah 84047
JAC 9.12.94

PRINTING HISTORY
First Printing 1995

ISBN: 1-56901-410-8

NPI books are published by Northwest Publishing, Incorporated,
6906 South 300 West, Salt Lake City, Utah 84047.
The name "NPI" and the "NPI" logo are trademarks belonging to
Northwest Publishing, Incorporated.

PRINTED IN THE UNITED STATES OF AMERICA.
10 9 8 7 6 5 4 3 2 1

ACKNOWLEDGMENTS

The author wishes to acknowledge the support and encouragement of the many individuals who have assisted him in the production of this book.

To my best friend, wife, confidante, and partner, Polly Wilde...thanks for putting up with me. I love you.

With out the love and support of my parents and family, none of this would have been possible. Thanks Mom, Dad, John, Jim, Lyn, Lee Ann, Jo Ann, Joey, Jim, Doug, Johnny, Heather, Megan, Rachel, Tari, Angi, Missy, Ben, Brehan, Josh, Chad, Holly, Brooke, April, Alissa, Drew, Donna, Mel, Amy, Dave, Andy, Melanie, Danny, Sally, Tom, Benjamin, and Jonathan. Whew!

An extra-special thank you goes to Chad Bulman for the great illustrations.

Special recognition goes to Donna Albright, whose insightful editing has greatly improved this work.

Thanks also goes to my cats, Mosh, Spazmo, and Herb, who chose to show their support by taking turns sleeping on top of the computer during the many hours of work preparing this book.

To my friends at East Troy Community Schools, (especially Carrie Franzene and Dan Parr) thanks for helping me grow as a professional and as a person.

Finally, I would like to thank a twenty-seven-year-old male for giving me the greatest gift of all...a second chance at life! Please support organ donation.

ONE
America Faces a Crisis

Anyone who reads a newspaper or tunes into the evening news is constantly reminded of the staggering problems our nation faces. We have a debt of four trillion dollars that is climbing by millions everyday. If my math is correct, that comes out to about $16,000 for every man, woman, and child in America.

We also have a serious problem with crime. It is more dangerous to be alive today than in any previous era. You can't be certain that going to a fast food restaurant or post office won't be a one way journey. In the past we could at least feel safe in our homes, but like a $2.00 hair cut, that is a thing of the past. Until recently we could always jump in our cars and drive to relax or take a trip for a change of scenery. Now a sixteen-year-old with a semi-automatic weapon may tap on your window and ask you to step out of the car. We are locking up more people than ever before. However, those being released from prison don't seem to be any less dangerous.

Despite a declaration of war, drugs remain available. More individuals are using illegal drugs today than ever before. The drugs they are using are more addictive, easier to obtain, and much deadlier than in past years. Teenagers are experimenting with drugs at an earlier age than previous generations. While some indicators point to a decline in the use of certain drugs, such as cocaine, we still have a problem. I work in the public schools...I see and I hear and trust me, we still have a problem!

Teenage pregnancy, racism, infant mortality rates, and the environmental disasters are serious problems. I could probably fill half of this book discussing the state of the nation, and we all would feel mildly depressed, but that's not the point of this book.

The deficit, crime, and drugs are all serious problems, but I propose they are not our most serious. **Our most serious problem in America today is that we are wasting millions of young minds.** Far too many of our children are failing to reach their potential. Too many of our children are under-achievers. They are losing interest. They are giving up, they are dropping out. They are making poor decisions that they will never recover from.

One reason this is our most serious problem is that the deficit, crime, drug abuse, teenage pregnancy and other serious problems are, at the very least, related to, and often times a direct result of school failure. A recent study reported that the lack of a high school diploma will cost an individual approximately $250,000 in lower wages over the course of a lifetime. The cost in human terms could be even greater.

Another reason the failure to maximize our youth's potential is our most serious problem is whether they like it or not, these future generations are going to be forced to deal with the problems we leave behind. Will they be prepared to deal with a fast moving, complicated, global society that requires increasing sophistication simply to survive?

Now, for the good news. **We can make a difference!** As parents, teachers, counselors or concerned citizens, we have to make a difference. You have taken an initial step simply by deciding to read this book. By that act you are saying, "Maybe my child/student(s) could be doing a better job?" You are right, it is possible they could be doing better, and simply by acknowledging that possibility you've opened yourself up to change. I commend you for that because it takes courage, but I must warn you that to achieve real change you will need more than just courage. Understanding and overcoming school difficulties can be a daunting task indeed.

While the focus of this book is on academic underachievement, the general concept of underachievement can be applied to every man, woman, and child today. We all have some area(s) in our life where we have failed to live up to our potential. It doesn't matter how intelligent, gifted, diligent, talented or successful we are in other areas, the fact remains that all people have at least some area of underachievement. As Will Rogers aptly stated so many years ago, "Everybody is ignorant, only on different subjects."

Take a moment and consider the various activities you are involved in throughout the day. Think of an activity you find extremely frustrating; an activity you would do nearly anything to avoid. When you have no choice and are engaged in this task, do you give up easily? Do you feel somehow less than adequate because of your ineptitude? This activity is probably one in which you underachieve. It could be athletics, cooking, driving, public speaking, carpentry, or virtually any activity. For this author, it happens to be fixing things. I would rather do anything than get out my tools and attempt to fix something around the house. I am quick to anger when I can't fix something. I usually lack the patience to think through what needs to be done because I am in such a rush to finish. After a half-hearted attempt I usually proclaim, "This can't be fixed," and then denigrate myself for my inability to repair things.

The principles described in this book to overcome academic difficulties can be applied to any activity you would like to improve. The tasks may change but the principles will remain the same. For example, if I decided I really wanted to improve my ability to fix things I could start by trying to understand why I have difficulties fixing things to begin with. Once I have a clear understanding of my shortcomings as a "handy man," I might set up a formalized, structured plan to improve my weaknesses.

I could devote more time to various aspects of repair work until my skills improved. I could always hire someone who was better at fixing things to help me and learn from him or her. I could analyze my attitudes about repair work and try to replace self-defeating attitudes with positive beliefs. If I were willing to tolerate frustration and discipline myself, in all likelihood my skills in this ability would improve.

Human beings are amazing creatures with untapped potentials in many areas. With the right approach, we all have the ability to learn new skills or improve deficiencies. Academic difficulties can also be overcome. The primary difference between the above example and academic underachievement is that most adolescents are not motivated to improve their academic performance and they lack the where-with-all to do it alone. That's where you come in. They need your help!

One of my goals in writing this book is to help you determine whether your child or student is an underachiever. This may seem to be an obvious question, but it's more complicated than it seems. If your child is struggling, I intend to supply you with information regarding what can be done to help the student. I see many, many parents and teachers who have good intentions and who work diligently to help a student. The problem is they lack the information and know how to maximize the impact of their efforts.

This book will give numerous techniques to help the student with core academic skills such as reading, math, and spelling but it will hopefully go much deeper. Most underachievers have other factors holding them back that are unrelated to academics skills. Any book on underachievement that does not address these issues is woefully incomplete. Psychosocial factors typically related to the underachievement syndrome will be examined. Attention will also be paid to the relationship between academic failure and adult achievement or outcome.

For parents to get the most out of your child's teachers and school district you need to understand the manner in which a school operates. By the end of this book you will be familiar with such things as grade level equivalencies, standard scores, percentile ranks, learning styles, and numerous other educational concepts. Teachers and parents who read this book won't ever feel intimidated by psychologists and other professionals who speak with a lot of sophisticated jargon. As with any profession, educational specialists have their own "language," and communication between home and school is often complicated by this. There often is plenty of talking but little communication and understanding.

There will be practical advice on how to structure a routine at home that will assist parents and children. Hopefully, such information will maximize homework completion and minimize hair pulling and the gnashing of teeth. Information on behavioral contracts and ideas on finding outside assistance will be offered as well.

Now, let us begin our journey. The clock is ticking and there is much to do. The task will not be easy, but it is worth the effort. The costs of sitting by while a student continues down the path of failure are far too great. We have lost too many already who will pay the price of lower wages, boring work, and unfulfilled dreams. We must all decide now to dedicate ourselves to the needs of the children in our lives.

TWO
What Is Underachievement?

As stated earlier, on the surface, this seems like a simple question. Taken at face value, it actually is very easy to answer. It is student's ACHIEVING at a level UNDER their capability or potential. Simple! It gets a little more complicated when we take a step back and consider some broader issues.

For example, are all children who score below their current grade placement underachievers? If we looked at a typical class of twenty-four second grade students and found seven scoring below second grade level in reading, could we say that they are underachievers? The answer is "no."

In another example, if we examined a class of twenty-nine high school freshmen (ninth graders) who were all scoring at a junior level (eleventh grade), could we conclude that **none** of these students are underachievers? The answer again is "no."

The reason we can not assume that the below grade level second graders and that the above grade level ninth graders are not underachievers is that we do not know what their overall ability or academic potential may be. If in the first scenario, the below grade level second graders had significantly impaired intellects (i.e. were mentally handicapped), they could not be considered underachievers. Even if they were a full year behind their current grade placement (i.e. reading at a first grade level), they still might be performing at an expected level given their academic potential. Conversely, if the freshmen who are performing at a junior level were extremely gifted intellectually, we might predict that they would be even further ahead. By definition, even though these students are performing two years ahead of their current grade placement, they could still be considered to be achieving below their overall potential. **Underachievement** can be defined as a discrepancy between students' **academic potential** and their **actual achievement.** More specifically then, **underachievement** is achievement **BELOW** a student's academic potential.

Some measure of intelligence is required to gather information regarding a student's overall achievement potential or academic capability. Most children receive group intelligence tests as part of the testing that is done each year. Some of the more popular group intelligence tests are the Otis-Lennon test and the California Abilities Test (CAT). It is much more reliable and valid to have a student's intelligence evaluated by a trained professional such as a school psychologist or psychometrist in a one-on-one setting. Even when an individual evaluation occurs there still tends to be disagreement and questions regarding the validity and usefulness of intelligence tests. What do those tests really measure anyway? What is intelligence? Aren't the tests culturally biased?

Measures of Intelligence

The following is not intended to be an in depth analysis of IQ tests but merely a brief review of some facts that might help teachers and parents better understand these controversial instruments:

1) Intelligence tests are designed to measure skills related to academic performance such as: perceptual motor coordination, abstract reasoning, short and long term memory, and general verbal ability.

2) Intelligence is generally considered to be multifaceted, but most intelligence scores are reported as a single number. Many times the total score is not as important as the numerous scores that provide information regarding a student's strengths and weaknesses.

3) Intelligence tests are developed with great care and revised several times before they are ever released onto the market for use with the public.

4) Intelligence test have variance or "error" built into them. They are not precise instruments like a scale that can give exact measures. That is why it is best to focus on the general level rather than the exact score when examining a student's performance on an intelligence test. This is why scores are often reported in ranges.

5) While intelligence scores can change somewhat over time, they tend to remain within the same general level for most students. A student who has average intelligence when evaluated in fifth grade is most likely to have average intelligence if tested again in eighth grade.

6) Intelligence tests do NOT measure **motivation** or **creativity** which can be extremely important in predicting academic success.

7) While many opponents of intelligence tests claim that cultural bias is inherent in such tests, empirical research has not supported this contention. Each question on an intelligence test is carefully evaluated to make certain that the question does not produce a disproportionate percentage of correct answers by males or females or by members of a particular ethnic class. If a question appears to discriminate between male and female respondents or between ethnic classes, it is not included in the final edition of the test.

8) Intelligence is but one measure of a student. While it is an important predictor of academic success, it is only one piece of information and should not be treated as the total picture of a student.

9) Intelligence tests can tell much more than just how well a child did on a test. To the trained professional, they provide a tremendous amount of information regarding a child's learning style and preferred approaches when faced with unique learning situations.

I have rarely met a parent who did not tell me his or her child was bright. This is even true of parents who have children who are mentally handicapped. They tell stories of how the child called the family cat a "tiger dog" or some other example of a time when the child surprised them with a response. In truth, a majority of children are of average intelligence and are not, by definition, "bright." The makers of the Weschler Intelligence Test for Children—Revised (WISC-R) (Weschler, 1974) have designated children scoring between 110 and 119 as bright or high average. This means that the upper one fourth of children could be considered bright.

One of the saddest things I see as a psychologist is when a family expects a child with an intelligence score of 88 to be a straight "A" student. It is simply not fair to students. They may be giving their best effort and will still be unable to meet these unrealistic expectations. Many times these parents say, "If he would just apply himself" or "She's just plain lazy." For these students, realistic grades may be mostly between C and B with an occasional A.

Vicki, an eleven-year-old, was referred to me by her parents because of academic difficulties. After looking over the student's cumulative folder I did not see any significant evidence that the student was struggling academically. She did not have a problem with attendance and the grades she had earned had been solid if not spectacular. I expected to find that she was struggling during the current school year. Vicki was in fourth grade. Many times students struggle between third and fourth grade when they are expected to operate with more independence. In meeting with her teacher, she explained that Vicki was doing satisfactory work in all her subjects. Her grades had been mostly in the C to B range. Since her parents had requested the evaluation, I decided to proceed with testing to see if there might be something to be learned about Vicki's learning profile that wasn't already known. After completing a battery of tests, I found her to be functioning with an intelligence quotient (IQ) of 90 and consistently scoring between the 3.2 and 3.6 grade level in reading, math, and spelling which is about where we would predict her to be, given the score she obtained on the IQ test I had administered.

The next step was to meet with Vicki's parents to explain the results of the evaluation. I explained to them that Vicki was scoring about one-half to one year behind her current grade level placement which was where it was predicted she would score. The parents looked at me like I had just given their daughter a life sentence. She was the youngest of four children who were all superior students, and they expected nothing less from Vicki. I remember saying, "But Vicki is not her brothers and sister." In effect, they expected Vicki to be an OVER-ACHIEVER.

Students with an IQ of 90 have less potential than three out of four classmates. Expecting them to be A honor role students is as fair as asking the parents to start going to classes along with third year medical students. All the effort the parents could put forth would, in all likelihood, still be insufficient. That's why it is important for parents to get information regarding the student's ability. It's the only way of making certain that the expectations for the student are in line with reality.

Let's assume for now that the student or students you are concerned about have at least average ability and are, in fact, achieving below potential. What do these students look like? What do they have in common? What factors or characteristics tend to be associated with underachievement syndrome?

Predictive Factors in Underachievement

When does the underachievement syndrome typically emerge? More specifically, at what age do students who are destined to have severe academic difficulties begin to struggle? One of the earliest studies to examine this question was conducted in 1960 by researchers Shaw and McCuen. The authors found that male high school underachievers scored below students in a comparison group as early as first grade. This difference reached a statistically significant difference by third grade and continued to widen from grade to grade thereafter. The female subjects in this study actually had higher grade point averages through fifth grade before declining. The decline continued and eventually reached statistical significance by ninth grade.

It is generally agreed upon by most professionals who study underachievement that, regardless of the age of onset, underachievement becomes more noticeable by late elementary grades. This is related to several factors:

1) Increase in homework—At early elementary levels most of the school day is spent practicing academic skills under the supervision of the teacher. The teacher gets an opportunity to observe the students' work directly and can give immediate reinforcement for successful work and correct any emerging problems or misunderstandings. By late elementary school students spend less time working in class and more time practicing their skills at home. With this increased independence the underachiever's performance may begin to decline. When left to work independently, they often lack the motivation and perseverance to complete a task.

2) No more "last minute rescues"—Many children, especially the brighter students, can be successful in early elementary grades without much effort. I've seen many second and third grade students take work home in their back packs and bring it back the next day without having completed it. In the few minutes they have between instructional periods they complete the work that is due. As the assignments become longer and increasingly complicated in junior high, they are

not able to continue these last minute rescues.

3) School is no longer new—During early elementary grades, school is still a new experience for students. Go into any kindergarten or first grade classroom and an overwhelming majority of children will tell you school is fun. They genuinely enjoy coming to school. Ask those same students if school is still fun by seventh grade and you'll get a different answer. In early grades, activities are kept short to accommodate shorter attention spans. By late elementary, students are expected to tolerate the frustration of tedious work. Let's face it, there are not many ways to make memorizing multiplication tables a fascinating endeavor. The assignments tend to get more demanding and less playlike.

Sex Differences

It is generally accepted that males are more likely to be designated as underachievers than females. Depending on which studies are cited, two or three males are classified as underachievers for every female.

Males are also more likely to suffer from a specific learning disability. Research also indicates that males are three to seven times more likely to be diagnosed with attention deficit hyperactivity disorder (ADHD). In fact, it is not an overgeneralization to say that females usually do better than males in school. This is certainly true if comparisons are made on grade point average alone as females consistently out perform males in this area.

Demographic factors also tend to be associated with the underachievement syndrome. Some studies indicate that underachievers are more common in larger families. Authors of such studies have speculated that with more children in the home there is less time and energy to be expended for academic support and monitoring. An only child certainly would have the opportunity to receive more time and attention than a seventh child. Whether or not the only child actually receives this time and attention is another question.

There also appears to be a tendency for underachievers to

be later born children with high achieving older siblings. This finding is in accordance with the theories of psychologists who postulate that birth order is an important factor in personality development. One of the cardinal tenets of birth order is that the achievements of older siblings will influence a younger sibling's choices. If an older sibling has distinguished himself or herself in academics, the younger sibling may choose another area to seek recognition to avoid the perceived competition with the older sibling. The threat of not measuring up to the past accomplishments of an older brother or sister is believed to be too anxiety provoking. The younger sibling either consciously or unconsciously heads out in a new direction. There are numerous examples where an older sibling was a straight "A" student and the younger sibling was a star athlete or vice versa.

A majority of studies find that underachievers are more likely to come from single parent households. Authors of these studies theorize that the stress of divorce could have a negative effect on the student's motivation and ability to concentrate. It is also possible that the decline in academic performance may be influenced by the decrease in time and attention to school related issues by the remaining custodial parent.

It is important to realize that none of the above mentioned factors can predict underachievement with 100% accuracy. Research like this presents the result of the investigation of GROUPS of students and may or may not be true of an individual student. Don't forget that there are thousands of 1) males from 2) large families who were 3) later born children with high achieving older siblings from 4) single parent households that are NOT underachievers! Conversely, there are plenty of 1) females from 2) small families who were 3) first born from 4) intact families who are underachievers.

Long Term Effects of Underachievement

One of the most extensive and ambitious studies of underachievers ever attempted was conducted in 1981 by Otto, Call, and Spenner. The authors contacted over 6,599 subjects who had been identified as underachievers as juniors and seniors (in the years 1965–66) thirteen years after high school. The authors found that underachievers were less likely to finish college and completed fewer years of post-secondary education than achievers of the same mental ability. Underachievers were almost twice as likely to attend vocational or technical school, but only half as likely to attend a college or university. Thirteen years after high school, underachievers held jobs of lower status than achieving students of the same mental ability. Underachievers held jobs of equal status with students who earned similar grades but were not considered underachievers as their grades matched their abilities.

Underachievers earned less money after high school than did achieving students of the same ability. Underachieving males earned $.76 less per hour than achieving students of the same ability which translates into 7.7% less pay. Underachieving females earned $.73 less per hour (12.2% less pay.) Underachievers held more jobs in the thirteen years following high school when compared with students with similar mental abilities. This fact lends support for the premise that underachievers have a difficult time tolerating frustration. When a job becomes frustrating or boring, the underachievers "bail out" just as they learned to do while enrolled in school.

Perhaps the most striking finding in this study was that underachievers were 50% more likely to divorce in the thirteen years following high school. This percentage was higher than either comparison groups (i.e. students who had similar mental abilities and students who had similar grades).

Do Underachievers Catch up?

Some underachievers did eventually catch up educationally and occupationally to students who had similar potential intellectually. It was noted however that underachievers who were two or more grade levels below expectancies did not catch up with students with similar abilities. These students only attained educational and occupational levels consistent with students with similar grade point averages. McCloskey, Evahn, and Kratzer noted that if a student is below expectations by only a grade or two, comes from highly educated parents, and possesses self-confidence he/she is much more likely to catch up. Without these characteristics, it appears underachievement is a relatively permanent condition.

Now that the commonly occurring demographic features and long term effects of underachievement have been examined, it is time to turn our attention to the psychosocial features of this group. What do group members have in common regarding the structure of their personality? What are the dynamics of their interactions with the world around them? Are there many types of underachievers or a single set of descriptors that pertains to all?

Low Frustration Tolerance

The most common characteristic in underachievers is that an overwhelming majority suffer from low frustration tolerance (LFT). LFT can be defined as an unwillingness (not an inability) to tolerate frustrating events. Anyone and everyone can tolerate frustration because we simply have no choice but to deal with it. There are times when we've all been stuck in the slowest moving check out line at the grocery store, and in order to purchase food we had no choice but to tolerate it. Being stuck in traffic is another frustrating event that at times is unavoidable. On the other hand, there are situations that are frustrating, but the possibility for avoidance or escape is possible. Doing homework is a classic example. A student always has the choice of closing the book! There may be consequences later, but the book can always be closed and the T.V. can be turned on. When stuck in traffic it is possible (but highly unlikely) that you would actually pull your car to the side of the road and start walking.

When one considers that school involves many frustrating events, it is easy to see how LFT can be a problem. It is virtually impossible to be successful in school without having the ability to tolerate at least a moderate amount of frustration.

In the learning process, there is typically a point between partial understanding and mastery of a concept that is very frustrating. That point comes when we don't quite "get it." Underachievers reach this point and simply give up. They bail out at this crucial moment where, if they could persevere for just a few more seconds, things would clear up. The difficult thing about breaking this tendency is that it feels good to get out of a frustrating situation. In effect, it is rewarding to give up. They have learned to give into immediate gratification, but will pay the price later. Some students never learn to delay gratification.

The ability to tolerate frustration may not seem like an important factor but I believe the **ability to tolerate frustration and delay gratification are the most important factors in predicting personal success.** Think of all the things that are worth having that you can obtain quickly and easily. It doesn't take long to finish that list does it? Now reverse the equation and think of the things that take time and are frustrating to acquire; professional degrees, successful businesses, nice homes, and most significant successes take time, effort, and dedication. Along the way there are inevitable set backs and numerous disappointments but to reach an important goal or obtain a certain level of success, you have to refocus yourself and keep working. Students who suffer from LFT have not learned this lesson.

The pattern of avoiding frustrating situations becomes hard to break and not only contributes to underachievement but affects virtually every area of a student's life. This type of thinking becomes ingrained in the student and works into their internal dialogue or "self-talk." Another way to think about self-talk is that "little voice" we hear in the back of our head or in our "mind's ear." Everyone talks to himself or herself virtually all the time whether they are aware of it or not. This self-talk contains the personal philosophies about the world that guide our behaviors and influences the decisions we make.

As a psychologist, I counsel underachieving students because, as I have stated earlier, many of the causes of underachievement have more to do with psychological factors than with academic difficulties. When working with these students, I use a specific method of counseling known as Rational-Emotive Behavior Therapy (REBT). REBT helps clients to focus on their self-talk and determine whether or not this internal dialogue is logical. Does the message lead to good results or bad results? Is there evidence to support the beliefs and ideas contained in this self-talk? If so, the beliefs are said to be rational. If the beliefs are not supported by evidence, the ideas are said to be irrational. Students who suffer from LFT all seem to hold one common highly irrational belief. They erroneously believe that "Life should always be easy and without frustration."

Obviously, life is not easy and contains a great deal of frustration. As I point out to my clients, life is actually spelled H-A-S-S-L-E. Don't get me wrong, it would be nice if life were frustration free but it isn't and probably never will be. Wishing or demanding that life be any different than it actually is does little good. It certainly does nothing to change reality.

LFT can manifest itself in many forms in school aged children. Educational psychologist William Knaus (1983) proposed that when the following behaviors are observed, LFT may be a primary or contributing factor:

1) Whining
2) Complaining
3) Day-dreaming
4) Lack of responsibility
5) Withdrawal or shyness

Knaus went on to make the point that many commonly occurring childhood problems such as eating disorders, poor impulse control, compulsive disorders, anxiety disorders, and conduct disorders all have one thing in common: low frustration tolerance. If a student exhibits tendencies associated with one or more of the above mentioned problems, and is also struggling with underachievement, I would suspect that LFT is, at the very least, a contributing factor to the student's difficulties.

As mentioned earlier, the idea that "Life should always be

easy and without frustration" is a belief at the core of LFT. However, there are other irrational ideas that many underachieving students hold that also interfere with their academic progress. Bard and Fischer (1983) examined a number of these irrational beliefs that lead to underachievement:

1) "Things will turn out OK whether I work or not" rather than the rational belief that "How things will turn out depends to a large extent on what I do. I can choose to avoid working but I realize that by not working I am probably creating a situation I will be forced to deal with at a later date."

2) "Everything should be entertaining and enjoyable and no unpleasantness should occur whatsoever" rather than the rational belief that "It would be nice if everything was entertaining but that is pretty unrealistic. There is absolutely no proof or evidence that unpleasantness should not occur."

3) "This is too hard...too much...too boring and I can't stand it" rather than the rational belief that "Nothing can be too hard because it is impossible to measure what 'too hard' means. No matter how hard or boring something might be, we can certainly stand it. To say we can't stand something means, literally, if we were to come in contact with this dreaded thing, it would kill us. No one has ever died from boredom."

Hopefully it is clear that if your child has this sort of internal dialogue or "tape" continually playing in his or her head, completing homework or paying attention to a teacher becomes very difficult. Once again, don't underestimate the impact LFT can have on academic achievement. Consider this scenario: It is 7:00 P.M. on a Wednesday evening and your fourteen-year-old is at the kitchen table trying to finish an algebra assignment. This "tape" is playing in her head:

"This is so BORING! The only thing more boring than doing this is listening to Mrs. Jaos explain it. Who could blame me for daydreaming about cheerleading practice. Besides, I shouldn't have to do this. What good is it going to do me? It's too hard. Following all the X's and Y's. Oh, who cares. I can always do it tomorrow in study hall."

Study hall is second period and, wouldn't you know it, the

homecoming float needs work. The end result will probably be an incomplete assignment.

How can you improve your child's ability to tolerate frustration? It's not easy and in all honesty, might be better left to a professional who has experience working with such matters. What you can do is point out the consequences of her decisions but to do so in a mean or sarcastic manner would be counter productive. When the student is grounded for poor academic work or missed assignments, trace the problem back to when they originally made a poor decision. The parents can explain in a calm, matter-of-fact fashion that it wasn't Mrs. Jaos's fault that the student chose not to study for the mid-term examination. It was her choice to go to the movies instead and put off studying. This may sound like lecturing but when it is done fairly and out of concern (instead of anger) the child is more likely to listen.

Another intervention that might be effective is to simply ask the student if he or she believes some of the earlier mentioned beliefs such as "Life should always be easy and without frustration." If the student says, "No" explain that you asked because his or her behavior suggested it. Putting off assignments and not studying seems to indicate that a student does believe "Life should always be easy and without frustration." Ask the student to explain why the above-mentioned idea is not true. Finally, ask them what the long term results would be if a person lived by the belief that "Life should always be easy and without frustration." At the very least you'll spend some additional time talking with your son or daughter, and that's something we all could do more of anyway!

If your student(s) do believe "Life should always be fair and without frustration," ask them for proof or evidence that this idea is true. See if they can make a connection between this belief and the problems they are having in school and other problems they may be having outside of school.

If some of you are concerned that this is bordering on "amateur psychology hour" you are absolutely right. That's why it might be a good idea to work with a professional counselor. I'm reluctant to recommend that wholeheartedly because the emphasis of this book is on what you can do as a parent or teacher to help the underachieving student. However, there are occasions where outside assistance is warranted.

There is one final technique for helping your child overcome difficulties with LFT. See if you can recognize when "Joshua" is talking to himself (i.e. when his "tapes" are playing) about "how boring or stupid school work is and how it shouldn't be so hard." Try to get him to interrupt this dialogue and then substitute a new thought. For example, just repeating a simple phrase like "I can do it" can be extremely beneficial. It gives the student self-confidence but more importantly, it blocks out all the negative self-talk. Following is an example of how you might help your student "switch tapes."

Adult: What are you working on there, Joshua?

Student: Science.

A: How is it going?

S: Not very good. I don't really like science. It's boring.

A: You know what? Every class has some parts to it that are more fun than other parts. Not every assignment can be fun and interesting.

S: I suppose you're right, but I still think this assignment is especially stupid.

A: Is that what you are thinking to yourself right now while you are trying to work?

S: Yes, that's exactly what I'm thinking. This assignment is stupid, and I don't know why I have to do it.

A: Can you agree with what I just said a minute ago that all classes will have assignments that may not be as interesting as other assignments?

S: Yes.

A: Then let's assume this is one of those assignments and what you need to do now is work through it the best way you can. Do you think that telling yourself "This assignment is stupid and I don't know why I have to do it" will help you do a good job or make it harder to do a good job?

S: I think it just makes me hate doing it that much more.

A: You're exactly right. What would happen if you told yourself something like this, "I can do it even if I think it's boring" or "I can deal with this even though I don't like it?"

S: I'd probably have a better attitude.

A: Do me a favor and when you hear yourself thinking how stupid this is try stopping yourself and thinking something else like "I can deal with this even though I don't like it." It will be sort of our experiment.

While LFT is a common component found in many underachieving students, it is certainly not the only identifying characteristic these students have in common.

Manipulation

Most underachievers are masters at manipulation because they have to be. Without being able to con and trick others, they would be unable to avoid being held accountable for their actions. Many underachievers are bright and they have the ability to use their intelligence in devious ways. Even at an early age they understand the key to being successful in the manipulation game lies in three little words: DIVIDE AND CONQUER. They seem to understand that if they can keep the home and school from combining forces they can avoid most of the negative consequences. At the very least, they can delay the impact of these consequences until a later date.

These students divide and conquer using whatever means necessary to keep home and school at odds. They often have an advantage because both parents and teachers are frustrated and feel somewhat responsible for the student's failure. Parents and teachers usually feel more responsible than is appropriate. When this is the case, the stage is set for a good deal of blaming and finger pointing as the school blames the parents and the parents blame the school. At this point the child has managed to divert attention away from himself or herself and tremendous energy is spent determining who is most at fault.

For example, Billy, a seventh grader, is struggling with a science project and the parents are trying to help. The child tells the parents, "The teacher didn't tell us how to do this. She just said we had to do a project about earth science." The parents then spend twenty minutes berating the teacher for not providing enough information regarding the guidelines for the project. They go on with this tirade belittling the teacher, the school, and the overall quality of instruction their tax dollars are financing.

Truth be told, the teacher has explained in great detail that the project can either be a collection of fall leaves, insects, or fossils. She has provided numerous handouts regarding her expectations for these projects and they have discussed previous projects she deemed to be exceptionally well done. Mrs. Tellefson even brought in several projects for students to see firsthand. Every class period for the past two weeks has started with an opportunity for students to ask questions regarding their projects.

From the parents perspective, the extent of the teachers output for this project was, "Do a project!" If, as a parent, you find yourself in this situation call the office the next morning and ask to speak with the teacher. If you are not certain that the information you are receiving is accurate, it is time to speak directly to the teacher. One other point, and this is an important point, **try not to be critical of a teacher or school in front of your child.** This simply does nothing to help the situation and sends a very negative message to the child regarding education in general. The students also learn that they *can* divide and conquer and as a result, this behavior will be repeated in the future. If you are dissatisfied with the school or the teacher, by all means, communicate your concerns to the proper personnel. Simply do it in private.

Another common example of dividing and conquering, with a slight twist, might go something like this:

Naomi, a ninth grader, has been failing to turn in her

biology assignments. The assignments consist of cutting out and pasting pictures of various organs in their correct position on a chart of the body. When asked by her teacher why these assignments were not being completed and turned in on time Naomi responded to the teacher, "My parents say it's stupid for a ninth grader to be working with scissors and glue." The teacher would, no doubt, be somewhat embarrassed and hurt as would many other professionals when their judgment is questioned. This is especially true when the teacher is questioned in front of twenty-eight ninth graders. The teacher might think, "Fine. She's not my daughter and it's not my grade. They're welcome to come in here and teach biology any time they want." However, after a moment passes the teacher regains composure and says to the student, "Would you do me a favor and have your parents call me because I'd like to discuss this with them." Naomi agrees and heads off to P.E. The truth of the matter is that Naomi's parents said no such thing because they don't have any idea what Naomi is doing in biology class. Naomi's handouts for this assignment are in the bottom of her locker. Does Naomi pass along the message to her parents to call the teacher? Of course not. The teacher doesn't hear from the parents and figures, "Well, it's not my responsibility. If they have a concern they know where I can be reached."

Let me alert you to the proverbial "oldest trick in the book," a trick that I'd guess 99% of students have used at one time or another.

Mother: How was school, Johnny?

Johnny: Fine.

Mother: Do you have any homework?

Johnny: No, I did it at school.

Mother: That's good. How about some milk and cookies?

Johnny: Sure, Mom.

Of course Johnny has homework but he knows he can pull the wool over mom's eyes with this tried and true classic. If we are all *brutally* honest most of us will admit that we all used this trick once in a while. So, if we all did it, why do we all fall for it? There's a simple way to put an end to this caper. Ask Johnny if you can see his homework to which he'll reply, "I left it at school." You should say, "From now on I want to see your homework every night."

The following night I virtually guarantee Johnny will "accidentally" forget to bring home his work. At this point it's a good idea to attach some consequences to Johnny's forgetfulness. If he has a standard bedtime, try moving it up by a half an hour as a reminder to bring his work home the next day. Don't be surprised if he forgets his homework again the next night just to see if you are serious about this threat of an earlier bedtime. It's very important to never make a threat you aren't willing or able to follow through on. If you're not willing to do it...don't say it!

One thing you can be sure of is **children want to know the rules.** They want to know where parents and teachers are going to draw the line. In other words, kids WANT limits. That seems to surprise some people, and it's easy to understand why, the way children will fight tooth and nail against rules. They will whine, complain, curse and damn their "overprotective" parents and teachers for their "stupid rules." Don't be fooled. They are secretly appreciative of rules because down deep they know rules are there because you love them and are concerned about them. As a teacher they know you set high expectations because you really want them to succeed. These rules send the very important message, "I care about you enough to take the time and effort to make sure you are doing things the right way." It's a shame they will probably never give you the satisfaction by saying, "Mom, Dad...Thanks for not letting me slide by." I hope they do take the time to thank you, but if they don't, know that they do appreciate your concern and support. I know they do because dozens of kids have told me during our counseling sessions.

Some children grow up as free spirits coming and going as they please. Not only do they not have a curfew, their parents often do not even know where these kids spent the night.

These are the children who tell your children how "cool" their parents are and brag about their freedom. I also know that most of these children grow up feeling very insecure. They've got the haunting feeling that they simply aren't worth caring about. They usually think their must be something bad about them and they are not worth the time and trouble to discipline. Also, these students usually have abysmally low frustration tolerance. How could they learn to tolerate frustration when they have had to face so little?

So if your adolescent is telling you what an overprotective monster you are for making them come in at a reasonable hour and bring their assignments home to be checked, pat yourself on the back. You're probably on the right track and, yes, it is worth the headaches!

The Work of Avoiding Work

There is an unusual paradox regarding the effort an under-achiever is willing to put forth to avoid work as opposed to the effort required to complete work. This is probably because they don't view avoiding work as work at all. To the classic manipulative underachiever, this type of activity is a game. Unfortunately, it's a game a good many play exceptionally well.

I remember a student who hated doing his spelling. His first attempt to get out of completing his spelling homework was to cut the corners off of the pages on his spelling workbook so he could claim he didn't know what his assignment was that day. The parents actually thought this was amusing. The teacher did not, and made the student come in during recess and renumber the entire book. I applaud the teacher for applying logical consequences for inappropriate behavior.

The same student took the spelling book home and lost it. The teacher called the parents (after first taking everything out of the student's desk to make certain it wasn't buried) and asked them to look at home. The parents turned the house inside out but could not find the workbook although they knew it had been at home because they had seen it. About a year later they found the book hidden inside a removable panel in their basement. What a creative mind! He hid the book so it was extremely unlikely it would ever be found. If it weren't for the water heater breaking down the parents never would have found it. Rather than just throwing it in the river he kept it close at hand just in case the punishment for losing the book would have been too great. If that were the case the book could magically appear at home or at school. Imagine if the student ever decided to channel that creativity into other areas. There might be a Nobel Prize out there with his name on it!

One of the things I do as an educational psychologist is observe students in their classrooms to see if I can gather information as to why they are not being successful. When I can focus on one student as opposed to twenty-five students, sometimes I can pick up on little things a teacher might miss.

One day I was observing a student who had been a concern during every year from first grade through fifth. He was bright but continually struggled due to missed assignments and other avoidable problems. He never seemed to have a pencil or paper (or his book for that matter). This day he had approximately forty-five minutes of independent seat work to complete a math assignment. The teacher was leading a reading group and the rest of the class was busy either with their math or other written assignments. As I watched this student I observed that he had his book open, paper and pencil ready, and gave every impression that he was working on the assigned problems. It's important to note that he was not bothering anyone. He got out of his seat on one occasion to sharpen his pencil. The amazing thing is that during that forty-five minutes he completed no math. The student simply sat quietly with his pencil near the paper and did nothing. He looked around the room on occasion and I assume he day dreamed for part of the time but he did not complete a single problem. Imagine the effort involved in coming to school, day after day, and fooling your teachers by looking very much like you were working but not actually completing any assignments. I am certain he could have done his assignment in fifteen minutes and spent the remaining thirty minutes doing something more enjoyable. According to the teacher, he had the skills to do the assignment. This was not a case of the student not knowing how to complete the work and being too shy to ask for help.

How did the teacher handle this? When it came time to turn in the assignment, the student told the teacher he didn't have it done. The teacher said, "Well, it's due first thing tomorrow morning. You'll have to take it home." The assignment never did get completed.

Disorganized

Many underachievers are extremely disorganized. These students are genuinely disorganized, but not like the child who manipulates a teacher by purposefully forgetting books. They continually lose assignments, books, and other important items. They spend a good deal of time and energy on an assignment and forget to hand it in to their teacher. If you cleaned their desk you'd likely find a dozen partially completed worksheets, three permission slips for field trips, and last week's check for lunch tickets. Many children need help getting organized, but these children REALLY need help.

As was stated earlier, many of these underachievers (especially females) first run into significant difficulties in junior high. During elementary school, when they have one teacher, they usually do fairly well. With a single teacher for all academic subjects they are monitored closely . The teacher knows exactly what they need to complete and with guidance, these students usually do reasonably well.

In the middle school where students have six or seven teachers, no single teacher has a sense of "ownership" over the student. They feel as though they only have the student for forty-five minutes a day just like everyone else. The student is their responsibility for one class and besides, they have 145 students and can't be overly concerned with any one student. To a certain extent, the teacher is correct. Eventually there has to be a shifting of responsibility from the teacher to the student and junior high is a reasonable place to start. The difficult part comes in finding a balance between supporting and "spoon feeding" the student. They have to learn to be independent, but some students require more support to make this transition.

How can we help them get organized? There are several simple things which can have an impact on the student's successes and failures. Perhaps the most important thing is to get the student an assignment notebook. Any small notebook pad for 49¢ is adequate. The student is to write down every assignment in this notebook along with the date the assignment is due. Before students can complete assignments, they have to know the assignments.

Students can also benefit from a "trapper keeper" or some type of folder for each class. One of these files in the folder should be for assignments that need to be turned in. Getting six separate folders would only promote disorganization. The trapper keeper with six folders should be carried to every class. Most trapper keepers also have a place to carry paper and pencil so the student will be reasonably well-prepared. The best way to help the student get organized is to simplify things for them. That way they have less to remember and can concentrate on their real job…learning.

Insecurity

Most underachievers are insecure regarding their ability to compete with their classmates. They are afraid they can't reach the expectations of their parents and teachers. In truth, they actually might be able to, but it's unlikely they will take the risk to find out because the threat of failure is perceived to be too great. This is another example of a paradox that seems to be quite common among underachievers. If the threat of failure is too great, why are they failing? If they really were afraid of failure, wouldn't they do anything and everything in their power to avoid failing?

What needs to be understood is that there is no sense of failure when a student does not put forth a legitimate effort to pass. If a student doesn't turn in an assignment, never opens a book, and doesn't study for tests, it's not a threat to their self-esteem to fail. Of course they failed. The outcome was never in doubt. What student could pass with such an effort? It's as if the underachiever is saying, "You can't blame me for failing. I didn't try."

Now consider the students who work diligently to turn in every assignment. They study for the examinations and even ask the teacher for extra credit assignments to make up for lost points. It's not as easy for these students to brush off failing. They have invested a great deal of time and energy but still haven't managed to meet the minimum requirements to receive credit in a class. While the student who doesn't try believes, "Failing for me proves nothing because I didn't try," the student who worked hard believes, "Failing proves how stupid I am."

There is a fundamental error in reasoning here. The belief being implied is that, "My overall value as a person depends on my successes or failures." People often make this mistake which is an overgeneralization from an individual's behaviors to his or her inherent worth as a human being. That is, many people foolishly believe that their actions can somehow prove something about their overall value. In the case above, the student believes, "Because I failed, it proves I'm stupid and if I'm stupid, I'm totally no good as a person." This type of overgeneralization is very common and can be applied to many other scenarios in our culture that occur everyday.

"Because I was rejected it proves I'm unlovable."

"Because I was laid off it proves I'm a rotten worker."

"Because I'm overweight it proves I'm worthless."

Logically, none of these beliefs make sense. Let's examine them in closer detail starting with the original, "Because I failed it proves I'm stupid and if I'm stupid, I'm totally no good as a person."

Failing proves nothing about a student other than the student did not earn a passing mark. It certainly does not prove a person is stupid even if he or she gave his or her best effort. No one is stupid, even though we all at times act stupidly. We eat unhealthy foods, fail to think situations through, put things off, and make ridiculous remarks. Even though it is true that we act stupidly, for someone to be stupid they would have to act stupidly 100% of the time which is impossible.

As for the second part of the belief ("If I'm stupid, I'm totally no good as a person"), this is also an irrational overgeneralization. It's impossible for people to be "no good" no matter what they say or do. Someone's accomplishments can't make a person worthwhile and failures can't make someone worthless. Everyone has a life and whether they realize it or not, they are the only ones able to find enjoyment and happiness. That makes each one of us very worthwhile and very valuable....to ourselves!

Locus of Control

Who is responsible for the final outcome in an academic situation? Who has control over the end result? The answer to these questions is that the **individual with responsibility and control is the student.** The teacher is not responsible for the student's grades nor do the parents have control over the ultimate success or failure in school. The fact that students control their own destinies seems clear to adults but to whom or what does the underachieving student attribute his or her successes and failures?

Rotter (1962) was one of the first psychologist to explore this question. He classified individuals along a continuum regarding their perceptions of control over end results. Rotter found that individuals divided into two broad categories regarding their perceptions of control: 1) **internal locus of control**—those individuals who believe that they are largely responsible for their successes and failures and 2) **external locus of control**—those individuals who believe that factors other than their efforts are largely responsible for their successes and failures. No one is purely internal or external in regards to his or her locus of control. As stated earlier, everyone falls somewhere on a continuum.

Underachievers tend to be both internal and external depending on the outcome. If underachievers fail an important task and have genuinely tried they have a tendency to internalize the failure. "I really tried to do a good job this time and I still failed. What a stupid jerk I am," is the type of attribution the underachiever makes. Students attribute their failure to their inadequacies.

When they get a good grade on a test or turn in a really well done assignment, they externalize or attribute their success to factors outside their control. "Man, did I luck out on that math test," is their reaction. These students seem to want the worst of both worlds! When they succeed it is not because they are capable but is usually credited to luck or some other external factor and when they fail, they take full credit. The above mentioned dynamics would help explain their tendency to avoid giving a strong effort on tasks they are uncertain about. If they try hard and fail, they feel responsible but if they do little or no work and fail, they feel as though they can not be blamed because they didn't try.

Passive-Aggressive

There are underachievers who will use school as a tool to bother and annoy their parents. The student has received the message loudly and clearly from the parents that, "School is important. Education is a priority. We value education and you should do well in school." The child may even agree with them and believe that education is important. However, children and adolescents have other motivations that will interfere with the best laid plans of their parents. **One of the most important and dominating goals for most adolescents is to annoy the hell out of their parents!** This can extend beyond parents, and usually does, to all authority figures, but since the parents are the ultimate authority figures, they usually bare the brunt of this rebellion. Many times such behavior has to be passive in nature because parents still control a majority of the "good stuff." Parents still control curfews, allowances, and car keys. As much as some adolescents would like, few will actually tell their parents to go jump in the lake. Acting in such an openly defiant manner toward their parents will probably bring a guaranteed punishment such as a grounding. It might be more accurate to say some adolescents will try telling their parents to go jump in the lake to see their reaction. If as a parent or teacher you allow this behavior to go unpunished, then you probably are experiencing it on a fairly regular basis. If you make it painfully clear to the student that you will not tolerate such behavior, and back it up by following through with an appropriate punishment, you probably will not experience full blown confrontations. What you will experience will be more passive in nature.

What is passive-aggressive behavior? I like to think of it as intentional behavior on the student's part intended to produce an unpleasant emotional reaction in parents and teachers such as irritation, anger, or embarrassment. For example, the young man who comes from the barber shop with a mohawk may honestly think the mohawk looks great but if he thinks his parents approve of the "new look," it is doubtful he would be wearing it. Any behavior that is moderately enjoyable or amusing to the teenager but will annoy a parent or teacher will automatically receive bonus points in the mind of most teenagers.

The student who is running with the "wrong crowd" may be doing so because of the reaction he's getting from his parents. Take a minute and think of the last few times you've been really irritated with your child. Could it be that he or she knew that the behavior would "push your buttons?" For a behavior to continue the student must some how be getting reinforced. If there appears to be no obvious reinforcement, consider the possibility that the student is enjoying bothering his or her parents and teachers.

Passive-aggressive behavior can be quite mild or can be taken to very serious extremes. I can think of examples where I believe teenage girls intentionally became pregnant in an attempt to hurt their dominating, controlling parents. These young ladies felt so angry and desperate that they struck out at their parents in a manner they felt would embarrass and humiliate their families. Thankfully, the passive-aggressive behavior patterns of most adolescents tend to remain on a fairly harmless level. It is much more common to use haircuts, earrings and clothing rather than incidents which will affect their families forever.

This may be surprising, but in most instances, passive-aggressive behavior is a sign of positive development in an adolescent. It's a sign that the teenager is trying to be his or her own person. It's an expression of a desire to be independent from the family. Adolescent rebellion, unnerving for parents and teachers, is a healthy sign when done in moderation. I'm highly suspicious of and somewhat concerned about the teenagers who live exactly as their parents want them to live. Some leave home and are not used to making decisions on their own and go completely over the edge with their new freedom and independence. They go away to college or move into an apartment and without rules put on them by others, they have a hard time setting their own limits. They have never had to live by their own rules. In effect, they have no internal control.

A fairly large percentage of teenagers rebel but don't flaunt it. They break rules, stay out too late, and commit other minor atrocities. It seems to be enough to them that they know they're rebelling. Years later they tell you that instead of staying over at Jenny's house, they traveled to the local college and partied at a fraternity. Be thankful for these kids because they are probably the easiest to be around. They still have a healthy ego and want to be independent but they aren't angry enough to come home with a skull tattoo. You are doing a pretty good job if you have an adolescent like this.

So parents who are struggling with a teenager in rebellion remember that it is a normal, healthy part of development. No, it's not fun but keep in mind it won't last forever and hopefully you and your child will live through this period. Don't forget that your teenager is acting like a teenager. To demand they act any other way is a failure to accept reality. Most teenagers are insensitive, egocentric, moody, unpredictable and difficult to deal with at times. That's the nature of the beast. So were we when we were that age although we may hate to admit it.

So what does all this have to do with underachievement? As stated earlier, when school is a priority in your home and that is clearly understood, your child can now use school as a weapon against you. I've found that many parents who also happen to be educators fall into this category. As the great French philosopher Albert Camus pointed out many years ago, the more you love something, the more you will eventually suffer because of that love. If school has been a large part of your life and you value education, what better way to hurt a parent than by failing in school?

What can be done to help students? They have to be held strictly accountable for their choices. When students chose to let school work slide, they need to suffer the logical consequences for that choice. When they do a good job they need to be rewarded. This may sound like an overly simplistic approach but to change an individual's behavior, there are basically two approaches: 1) you can make them work toward something or 2) you can make them work to avoid something. After all the theory and research on human motivation, attribution tendencies, and behavior modification, it boils down to these two options.

A crucial point that can't be stressed enough is that **a parent can't make a child do well in school.** No matter how much you try or what you do, it is ultimately up to your child. That doesn't mean give up and give in. Understand that the most important thing you can do is set realistic expectations for the student as well as administer positive and negative consequences depending on their behavior.

There is one last point for those of you who have had some training in psychology and are scheming of a way to outsmart your passive-aggressive teenager. It logically follows that if the child realizes you value education and he's using that as a tool against you, if you pretend to stop valuing education, maybe you can take away his motivation for underachieving and he'll start working. While this reverse psychology may work on paper , it will never work with your child. The worst thing you could do would be to pretend you just don't care.

First off, you'd never in a million years convince your child. They can't and won't forget all the talks about school and the passion you have for report cards and science projects. They'll see right through such a ploy.

The other reason this won't work is that it's easier not working than working. Given the choice, most students will watch T.V. instead of doing their algebra homework. This is absolutely true for students with a history of underachievement who may also have difficulties with low frustration tolerance and lack confidence in their academic abilities.

Having detailed some of the major psychological attributes of underachievers, it might be interesting to examine the characteristics of success oriented individuals as listed by Felton and Biggs (1977). It needs to be kept in mind that, just like a set of descriptors of underachievers, each of these qualities will not be found in all achievement oriented individuals.

1) Success oriented individuals prefer moderately difficult jobs (or moderately risky goals) as opposed to very easy or very difficult jobs, whereas underachievers tend to underestimate their abilities and set minimal goals. This tendency is also produced by the underachiever's fear of failure. A certain percentage of underachievers set unrealistically high goals and then berate themselves when they are unable to achieve those goals.

2) Success oriented individuals are generally more persistent as opposed to underachievers, with LFT, who give up prematurely.

3) They see themselves as responsible for their success as opposed to underachievers who have an external locus of control when it comes to success. The classic underachiever will attribute success to luck and failure to their own worthlessness. It is interesting to note that just the opposite occurs in success oriented individuals: they attribute failure to lack of effort or bad luck.

4) They work well under pressure as opposed to underachievers who put things off until the last minute but are then frozen by fear.

5) They are relatively independent from social pressure and tend to ignore group norms as opposed to underachievers who are insecure and have a greater desire to be accepted by their peer group.

6) They like to get feedback about their performance on tasks, and are able to modify their behavior realistically on the basis of that feedback as opposed to underachievers who do not enjoy being evaluated. They confuse their performance on a task with their overall value as a person. This overgeneralization makes evaluation dangerous and fearsome to the underachiever.

7) They have better abilities to delay rewards as opposed to the underachiever who has a difficult time delaying gratification. Success oriented people are able to consider situations in a longer perspective and are not overly focused on the here and now.

8) They think positively. They seem to focus on opportunities for success, rather than on the risk of failure as opposed to underachievers who evaluate their capabilities in a negative light. At their very core, they doubt themselves and their skills.

9) They value success. They are proud of their accomplishments as opposed to the underachiever who tends to minimize their accomplishments as they often feel these accomplishments are due to luck.

10) They are willing to take responsibility for the work they do; they want credit if they succeed and are willing to take responsibility for the consequences if they fail as opposed to the underachiever who fears failure and therefore gives only minimal efforts.

11) They seek out opportunities to compete with a standard of excellence as opposed to underachievers who generally fear competition.

12) They are generally realistic about their capabilities as opposed to underachievers who are poorer judges of their strengths and weaknesses.

THREE
Parenting Practices that Promote Underachievement

Due to a lack of information and understanding, parents can unwittingly contribute to their child's academic difficulties and underachievement. Parents have a tremendous impact on the values, beliefs, and ideals of their children. Whether they are aware of it or not, there is a continuous stream of data flowing out of parents communicating to their children. Students have an uncanny ability to read the subtle messages in this behavioral information. The wrong messages about school can have a negative effect on students' attitudes, and then on their academic performance. If you recognize some of these patterns in yourself and in your interactions with your children, be grateful. Now that you are aware of these behavior patterns you can consciously attempt to change them. Awareness is the first requisite before any meaningful change can take place.

Mr. and Mrs. Blame

As mentioned earlier, many underachievers are master manipulators and can divide and conquer with ease. They have managed to avoid being held responsible for their behavior by keeping the focus off themselves and keeping it on their teachers. In effect, they play both ends against the middle.

When there are difficulties at school, often both parents and teachers experience irritation, frustration, and anger. When a child is capable of doing an adequate job in school but is not doing so, everyone is losing and no one is happy. It is easy for both parents and teachers to start blaming each other. The teachers say, "If the parents would give us some support, we could turn this student around. I only have her one period a day. After all, she's their kid." The parents say, "Why don't they teach the kid? That's what they get paid for. After all, she's their student."

When parents criticize the school it very well may be justified. The school might not be doing everything possible to guarantee a quality education for the child. As has been previously stated, this criticism should not be made in front of the student. When students hear negative comments about the school and education in general, it only reinforces their negative attitudes toward school.

As a parent, you are the closest thing to a god your child will ever know. When a parent criticizes the school and blames the school for the child's difficulties, the child will believe it is the school's fault they are failing. Ownership for the problem is taken away from the child. The truth is that if a child is failing, it is partially everyone's fault. The school and parents could probably be doing more to help. The student could certainly be doing more and eventually will have to do more if he or she is to improve. All three parties (the child, school and parents) have a stake and it takes all three working together to be successful.

Here is a perfect example of how blaming the school and backing the child can turn out to be a disaster. A student was falling behind with his work in his sixth grade social studies class and was having to complete the work at home. He came to school one day and when the teacher asked him for the assignment he had taken home, he claimed he had lost it. According to the student, he had the assignment in his coat pocket and it must have fallen out on the way home. Even if the student did honestly lose the assignment that does not take away from the fact that the student is responsible for turning in the completed assignment on time. The student protested that the teacher was not being fair. The teacher explained that the rules were very clear and simple. The punishment for not turning in an assignment was to spend one noon recess period in detention making up the missing work.

The next day the student brought a note from home which read in part, "You are being very unfair to my child. If he says he lost the assignment then I believe him. He shouldn't be punished for making an honest mistake. Are you (the teacher) perfect and have never lost anything accidentally? Do not punish my child for things that are beyond his control."

From that point on the student knew that, right or wrong, the parent would back the child and not the school. As you might have guessed, more assignments were lost and the consequences for such irresponsible behavior never really fell squarely on the shoulders of the student. I honestly believe that the parent did not realize the damage he was doing by unconditionally backing the student. The end result was the undermining of the teacher's authority, and it gave permission for the child to pick and choose which rules he was going to follow.

Mr. and Mrs. Permission to Fail

Parents who suffered through school have basically two choices when it comes to what they are going to communicate to their children about school: 1) They can tell them school was hard and they hated every minute of everyday. The parents gave up on school at an early age and today think that school is a waste of time. 2) They can tell them school was hard but they wish they had tried harder. The parents now realize that school is the ticket to a better life and even though school is not always fun, it's extremely important. I hope you'll have no difficulties deciding which attitude will promote achievement and which will not.

The good news is that I'm confident that an overwhelming majority of you hold attitude # 2. Why else would you be reading this book?

Parents who openly express attitude # 1 are forgetting or failing to realize that their children identify with them. Children look up to their parents and want to be like them even if their behavior does not suggest they are learning from dear old mom and dad. When parents say, "I wasn't any good in school" they are laying the ground work for a son or daughter to follow in their foot steps. It is almost as if they are being given permission to be perform poorly because there is an unspoken message that follows the initial statement, "I wasn't any good in school." The unspoken portion is, "And I don't expect you will be either." Students perceive the unspoken part just as clearly as if the parent had said it, and this message gives them the green light to keep right on failing.

Expectations are so very important in predicting the success or failure in any endeavor. This is especially true when it comes to school. When students think they are going to succeed, they usually do. When they think they are going to fail, they usually do.

Not only are parent and student expectations in determining success important but teachers expectations can have a major impact on student performance as well. In a book entitled *Pygmalion in the Classroom,* a group of researchers wanted to determine the effects teacher expectations had on student performance. In the spring the authors of this book went into the classrooms the students would be in next year and erroneously told the teachers they had been doing some testing with the students they would be getting in the fall. They gave them a list of students they expected would show a real "learning spurt" during the next school year. They expected these students to surge ahead of their classmates. The truth of the matter was that the authors had done no testing on any of the students and had actually picked these so called "spurters" at random. There was nothing significantly different about these students from their classmates up to that point.

When they came back the following spring they found that the students they had designated as "spurters" had actually performed better than their classmates. They were described by their teachers as brighter than a majority of their classmates and their academic performance was higher. The only difference between the two groups of students was in the minds of the teachers. The expectation that the one group of students was going to perform more effectively than the other group made this expectation become a reality.

There is a lot of discussion and concern about a child's self-concept. It is important to realize that within the student there are many situation-specific self-concepts. They have a self-concept as an athlete, a self-concept as a worker, and a self-concept as a student to name but a few. When a child has a negative self-concept as a student, school work actually becomes more difficult. These students will not answer in class because their internal dialogue is telling them, "I'm probably wrong." They won't shoot for an "A" because they are thinking, "The best I'll do is a C." They won't try to plan a really great science project because their low self-concept tells them, "I couldn't do a really good project like some kids."

As parents and teachers we have a tremendous influence on a student's self-concept as a learner. As just discussed, when we set high but realistic expectations, students will try and rise to meet those expectations. The same is true for low expectations. When you expect little, you'll receive little.

A fascinating process occurs in all of us that partially explains this phenomenon. When a student holds the belief, "I'm no good in school," he or she feels more comfortable if the results support that belief. That is, if one expects to do poorly and does, he or she feels at ease with the results because the results are consistent with the expectations. When the results are inconsistent with the expectations there is a sense of uneasiness or anxiety. When a student is used to getting "C's" and then receives the highest score in the class, it can be anxiety producing because the results don't match the belief, "I'm no good in school." This phenomenon, known as "cognitive dissonance," doesn't appear to make sense until the underlying dynamics are examined. Logically it would appear that any student used to getting "C's" would be thrilled to get the top score in the class.

Have you ever heard someone being described as "programmed to fail"—the type of person who is making great strides toward succeeding and at the last minute does something to completely mess things up? I've heard others say about this type of person, "It's almost like they were trying to fail." The sad and peculiar thing is they were! The anxiety produced by the inconsistency between the belief, "I'll never win" or "I can't do well" and the reality that they were about to succeed is too much for them. They trip themselves up and return to a state where their beliefs match the results, namely failure.

In an underachiever who has a negative self-concept as a

learner, this dynamic takes place regularly. Once a student adopts a self-concept as a failure, it takes a lot of time and energy to change that negative self-concept into a positive view of oneself.

It seems like it should be possible to simply tell students that they are bright and can do well, and magically, their beliefs will change. The problem is that once they adopt this negative self-concept as learners, they reindoctrinate themselves with these beliefs literally hundreds of times a day. Numerous times everyday they tell themselves, "I can't do this" or "I'll never be able to understand fractions." This type of self-talk or internal dialogue occurs at a level they aren't even aware of most of the time. These "tapes" are buried but they play many times a day, everyday. That's why it is so hard to change a negative self-concept once it has been established.

The first necessary step is to be as positive as possible with the child. Students hear so many negative comments throughout the day and don't need to experience any additional derision. They do a fine job of deriding themselves with their own thinking most of the time and don't need assistance.

They also need to succeed. With success will come more success, and in time they will become less anxious about doing well. Eventually something magical happens. A little voice in the back in of the head whispers, "I can." For a long time all that voice ever said was, "I can't." Now that voice has changed, and the student has reached a most important turning point. It may not be immediately apparent when this change occurs, but it won't take long to discover something dramatic has happened to this student. Teachers will be saying things like, "Sara would never answer in class but lately she's getting more involved" or "Roger seems more willing to take a chance in class." Don't underestimate how important a victory it is when this transformation takes place. Parents and teachers need to enjoy it.

There was a little girl, Megan, I had a chance to work with a few years ago. She was a very bright child with an IQ of 125 which is almost in the gifted or genius range. Her potential was greater than nine out of ten students her age, and may have been even higher if it weren't for the fact that she had some learning problems. Megan was not a very good reader and had a difficult time remembering things. She had other strengths, however. She could understand verbal analogies better than most high school students even though she was in third grade. Megan had a way of making logical connections between things that was remarkable.

Her parents asked if I could help them understand why school wasn't going as well as it could have been. They would go over and over her spelling words, and she would still struggle. They would study for a social studies test, and her father would swear that when she went to bed the night before the exam she knew the information. She would somehow still do only reasonably well on the exams.

After evaluating Megan I sat down with her and her parents and explained that she did indeed have some memory problems that were probably interfering with her progress. I also suggested some techniques to help her more effectively remember what she had read. But the most important thing that happened that afternoon was that I explained to her what a bright little girl she was and what real strengths she had. I also told her that the types of activities they were doing in school would be changing. In a few years they would be expecting students to use skills such as abstract and analogical thinking. I told her she was as smart as most high school students in these areas even though she was only in third grade. I also told her that I really, truly believed she was going to do much better and that eventually she would be one of the very top students in her grade. As I said, a few years have passed but I did hear from Megan's parents recently. They said her grades had been steadily improving, and on the last report card she had earned straight "A's." They said the little hints I had given her about ways to improve her reading had helped her but what really made the difference in their opinion was the talk I had had with Megan. They said they could see that Megan really believed things would get better in the future. Is this an example of *Pygmalion in the Classroom*, or a fluke? I don't know for sure but I am convinced that whatever can be done to change a student's beliefs from, "I can't" to "I can" is worth trying. Nothing I know of will have a greater impact on a student than this change in attitude.

Mr. and Mrs. Inconsistency

I'm sure I'm not telling you anything surprising when I tell you that inconsistency leads to a lot of difficulties with your children and students. There are parents and teachers who are inconsistent and aren't aware of it. Inconsistencies give mixed messages to students that confuse them. Hopefully in this section we can examine a few ways to avoid inconsistency and the difficulties it can bring about.

People spend time and energy on things they deem important. If you really value having a sharp looking car, you spend time waxing and cleaning the car. If looking good at the beach is of vital importance to you, lifting weights and working out is probably part of your daily routine. If your child's education is truly a top priority, you probably spend time quizzing them for spelling tests, helping with homework, and numerous other activities that demonstrate that interest. You spend time and energy on the activities you think will maximize your child's chances of being successful.

Some parents talk about the importance of education but don't actually do anything to demonstrate their concern. The student knows this and as I've already said, you can't fool kids. You might be able to fool your boss, you might be able to fool your spouse (sometimes), but you can't fool kids!

At report card time parents may give lectures about the importance of working hard in school and are probably sincere. However, nothing takes the place of daily involvement in your children's activities . It takes the daily demonstration of concern to really convince your child that education is a priority.

If you value education and demonstrate this value, chances are your children will value education as well. As has been emphasized, your children identify with you. They tend to value and believe in the same things you do. But once again, it takes more than lip service. It takes real commitment. You may not even realize all the "school like" things that go on each and every day. These events are perfect for actively demonstrating to your child the importance of education. For example, when you are balancing the checkbook, get them involved by having them check some of your addition and subtraction. When you write a letter have them add a sentence or two to the letter. Read things that interest you out loud such as an article in a magazine or newspaper. Have your child help write down a list of things you need to shop for at the grocery store.

Parents also act inconsistently by failing to follow through on promises. If you state that each night from 7:00 to 7:40 p.m. there will be no activity other than homework and then two nights later let the child skip a night, what message are you sending? I'm not saying there never comes a time when an exception can't be made, but it's best if absolutes aren't stated. When parents and teachers speak in black and white terms and say things like, "Every night there will be two hours of homework done at this table," or, "Absolutely no assignment will be accepted late," you're setting yourself up and your credibility suffers.

If you've already made a blanket rule such as, "Every night from 7:00 to 7:40 P.M. there will be homework done," you could try softening the demand if the student has been keeping up with the work. Explain to the child that since things have been going well, only five nights, Sunday through Thursday, will be homework nights. If that means only 25 minutes is required to complete all the assignments then there will only be 25 minutes of homework that night. Also explain that if things keep going well there may be more reductions in the future, but that will only happen if things continue to improve. This type of negotiation or relaxation will please the student but will not undermine your authority. Make certain not to make such adjustments when things are on a down swing.

"EDUCATION AND LEARNING ARE THE MOST IMPORTANT THINGS"

Mr. and Mrs. Overly Involved

Occasionally a situation arises where parents become overly responsive to the needs of their underachieving son or daughter. The parents are so concerned and involved that their child's underachievement becomes their problem rather than the child's problem.

The child learns that by sitting back and playing the victim, the parents will come to the rescue. If they wait long enough and flounder enough, the parents will take over all the responsibility and basically do his or her assignment. A pattern is set. When homework time comes, the child will start the assignment by looking confused before stating emphatically, "I can't do this" or "I don't get it." The parent will come over and help the child with a problem or two and say, "O.K. now you do the rest." The child will wait the required 30–60 seconds with the obligatory puzzled look before saying, "I still don't get it." The parent may do a few more problems and leave thinking the child surely understands now. Once again the child asks for assistance and this time the parent thinks, "Well, there's only eight left. I'll just help with the rest so I know he gets it." The problem is that the student really doesn't learn anything about the assignment but did learn a clever way of getting out of homework.

These types of parents typically have some self-esteem issues of their own. The parents may be living vicariously through their children, which all parents do to a certain extent. As with most things, there's a limit to when this stops being acceptable and starts being a problem. It's as if the child's accomplishments become the parent's accomplishments. The child's achievements are more important to the parents than to the child. Somehow it's not the child's grades anymore but a direct reflection of the parent's value as a human being that is at stake.

Mitzi was a sixteen-year-old junior who was struggling in geometry. She happened to be a very talented athlete, and if she didn't pass geometry, she would be ineligible to participate in athletics. Rather than encouraging Mitzi to work harder in geometry, her parents set up a situation where they double-checked her work each night, which was fine. I do have problems however, with the parents fixing or "touching up" assignments with the correct answers when there were mistakes. How will students ever learn the really important lesson, which is that no matter what, they are responsible for themselves? The parents took that responsibility away from Mitzi and robbed her of an opportunity to learn this very important lesson.

If what I'm describing may be a problem in your home try to be as honest as possible about your motivations. Is it really a case of wanting the best education for your child or are your child's achievements a feather in your cap? That is not to say it is wrong to feel proud of your child for doing a good job. Remember, the child is the same child whether he or she is on the honor roll or not. Their grades are a reflection of how well they perform in a certain subject area—nothing more, nothing less. The grades don't measure the student's inherent value and they certainly don't measure the parent's value. Those lines can become blurry and get confusing at times but it helps to take a step back occasionally and get a reality check. Start with the question mentioned above, "What's my real motivation here?"

One final point before moving on, if you're going to be guilty of something, being overly involved in your child's education is not the most heinous crime ever committed. Being overly concerned and running the risk of taking responsibility away from your child is much better than showing little or no concern. It's much easier to slack off than try to push the stone up the hill from a dead start. The first step involves a willingness to admit there's a problem.

When you demonstrate the first few problems and the child asks for assistance, feel free to help but make certain the child is really trying to work through the problem. Point to an earlier problem that is similar and say, "What was the first step in problem one?" If the child says, "I don't know" (and they probably will) have them look over the example problem carefully and try applying that logic to a current problem. If they still don't seem to grasp the concept, redemonstrate on problem number one but make the student copy this step. By walking through the problem this way, the student is still responsible for the work on the current problem. This will take away the child's motivation to "play dumb" and attempt to manipulate the parent into doing the work. If the student gets the message, "I'll help you if you really need help but you'll actually be the one working" he will be more likely to ask for help only when needed.

FOUR
Teaching Styles That Promote Underachievement

Just as there are parenting practices that promote underachievement, there are also teaching styles that contribute to academic difficulties. While first and foremost, underachievement is a student problem, it is unwise to ignore the influence parents and teachers have on the student. As the major authority figures in the student's life, parents and teachers have the capability of either helping the student become a more responsible individual or allowing the student to continue to perform below expected levels by putting forth minimal effort. To a large extent, the course of action agreed upon by parents and teachers determines whether or not the pattern of academic failure will continue.

Before I continue I want to clarify what is meant by "teaching style." It refers to more than just a teacher's instructional practices or preferred way of approaching the material to be taught. Teaching style refers to a wide range of activities such as instructional techniques, discipline practices, policies regarding late work, and other important teacher controlled decisions.

If teachers have tremendous understanding of a subject matter but are unable to manage the behavior of students, their overall ability to reach the learners will be compromised. If teachers have strong skills with regards to discipline but are weak when it comes to asking high level questions, their educational impact will also be less than optimal. All of the above mentioned practices influence students' work habits and subsequently, their achievement.

The Overly Rigid Teacher

Each teacher falls somewhere on a continuum regarding a desire for order in a classroom. Some are comfortable with students being very active and moving around the room on their own accord while others desire a very controlled environment. The same comparison can be made regarding a teacher's willingness to allow for novel approaches to problem solving. Some firmly believe that there is one, and only one, way to solve quadratic equations. Any student who attempts to deviate from the "correct" procedure is criticized and encouraged to do things the "right way." Others allow for experimentation which tends to encourage and nurture original thinking.

It has been my experience that teachers who are overly rigid in their practices and philosophies are more likely to unwittingly contribute to underachievement. All students need structure and clear expectations regarding what is acceptable behavior and performance. The key is **to provide adequate structure while remaining flexible enough to promote creativity.**

As many underachievers are bright students, they naturally have unique ideas and novel approaches. When these ideas are rejected and students are criticized for such originality, it can lead to frustration, resentment, and eventual failure. If these same students are given latitude to use their creativity in a positive fashion they are more likely to apply themselves to the best of their abilities.

I remember a student who, in fourth grade, had a very difficult year. He was placed with a teacher who liked to do things by the book. There was little room for improvisation or divergent approaches. The student could not or would not accept that for every problem there was a right way to find the solution. He was the type who worked best when there were few rules and even fewer parameters regarding acceptable ways to find answers. Needless to say, it was a frustrating experience for both teacher and student. The teacher did his best to get the student to follow the steps. The student did his best to drive the teacher crazy.

The following year the student was placed with a teacher who was more relaxed as far as her expectations for following procedures. She was very comfortable with students using their own strategies as long as the quality of work was acceptable. One of her philosophies was that students should be challenged to find their own solutions to problems. These activities promoted original thinking which she clearly encouraged.

For example, students might divide into teams of four, and an assigned task would be to list all the possible uses for a spoon. To give the teams practice in math they would be given a set of numbers such as 2, 4, and 6. Using the four basic mathematical operations (addition, subtraction, multiplication, and division) they were to discover as many products or answers using just these numbers ($2 + 4 + 6 = 12$, $2 + 4-6 = 0$).

The above mentioned student thrived on these kinds of challenges. It allowed him to use his natural strengths and made school challenging for him. Needless to say, he had a more enjoyable year and did a much better job academically.

The overly rigid teacher also takes away the opportunity for a student to learn self-discipline. Helping students learn to be responsible for themselves is an important part of their overall education. When they learn to work independently, budget their time, and take care of themselves, students are in a much better position to transfer those skills to the responsibilities that await after graduation.

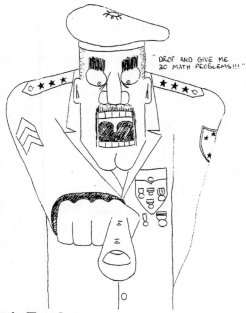

The Chaotic Teacher

Paradoxically, the lack of control in a classroom can also be detrimental to academic success. In much the same manner as overly rigid teaching practices can promote underachievement, chaos in the classroom also interferes with learning.

As already stated, underachievers are typically not the most self-motivated students in the classroom. Left to their own devices, they would much rather play than work. It is true they tend to be creative but often times the creativity they choose to explore has more to do with creatively avoiding work rather then creatively completing it!

Placed in a classroom that has few clear rules and expectations, underachievers flounder. They can easily give the appearance that they are engaged in constructive activities when they are wasting time. They will take the openness of the classroom as an invitation to dabble in one activity before moving to the next. Many will have a hard time completing any work or truly mastering a skill in such an environment. As stated earlier, what is needed is an appropriate balance. Ideally the student will not be forced to "toe the line" and quietly tolerate the standard "drill and practice" procedures. Underachievers rarely stand such routines due to their poor frustration tolerance. On the other hand, they need to be held accountable for their daily work and gently "pushed" by the teacher. Whenever possible it is best to give the underachiever the freedom they desire as long as they can appropriately deal with the independence.

For example, in an English class, an assignment might require a student to turn in a term paper. The project may not be due for several months. To simply explain the assignment and remind the students when it is due may seem reasonable, but it has been my experience that many underachieving students lack the ability to motivate themselves until the very last minute. A term paper can not be completed the night before it is due if it is going to be of decent quality. It has to be worked upon steadily over the weeks approaching the due date.

Sitting down individually with students and setting up a timetable for successful completion of the paper is an excellent way to help the students budget their time and avoid the last minute rush. This is especially a good technique if a student is often overwhelmed by the size of an assignment. By breaking the assignment into smaller components, the assignment seems to be more manageable.

Week 1: Select a Topic
Weeks 2–4: Researching the Topic
Weeks 5–6: Note Cards
Week 7: Rough Draft
Week 8: Editing
Week 9: Final Revisions
Week 10: Turn in Paper

This type of program can keep a student slowly working

toward the end product. It is also an excellent means of teaching the student that good results usually come through patience and perseverance. Some things can not be put off until the last minute no matter how talented a student might be.

The Angry Teacher

At one time or another we have probably all had experience with "the angry teacher," the teacher who is sarcastic, quick tempered, and seems to enjoy belittling students. This type of teacher is burned out. They were probably good teachers at some point in the past but they have lost the energy and drive to be a good teacher today. The demands of teaching, which are tremendous, have taken their toll and the students are the ones who suffer.

The effect the burned out teacher has upon brighter students is to shut them down completely. These teachers communicate quite clearly with a look or a subtle comment that they haven't got time for students who require additional energy and attention. They don't want questions from the class because they view these questions as unnecessary interruptions and as a personal affront to their skills as a teacher. They seem to believe that if a student doesn't understand a concept it reflects on their teaching abilities.

Many times you will find a battle brewing between the gifted underachiever and the angry teacher. The administration in a school district will call this a "personality conflict." The student usually loses this fight because in the end the teacher still has more power than the student. The teacher needs to remember who is the adult and who is the child. It is also important to realize on a daily basis that the school isn't here for teachers, principals, and psychologists...it's for the students.

If you believe your son or daughter is involved in a power struggle with a teacher it is a good idea to try and resolve the conflict one way or another as soon as possible. It is probably best to contact the teacher and arrange some over due "peace talks." Having the principal at this meeting is recommended. If you do run into a situation where the teacher is being unreasonable you're going to need the support of the teacher's superior. Hopefully, that won't be the case but it's important to remember that teachers are fully human and as such, have the right to have bad days, act selfishly, and be less than perfect...just like the rest of us.

The Bored Teacher

Perhaps the single most important thing a teacher can bring to a classroom is a genuine love of learning. All great teachers have this, and believe me, it can not be faked. Students can not be fooled and a teacher's true feelings about school and learning in general are communicated in many subtle ways.

Many times bored teachers discourage questions as well but not because they view questions as unnecessary interruptions but because questions may interfere with the preplanned lesson. It takes more effort to let the class explore new ideas and concepts than it does to simply go through the motions with a lesson they have taught a dozen times before. Students are more alive and interested when there are fewer boundaries, and they are allowed to creatively question a topic. **Sticking to the lesson as planned can be exactly what kills the natural curiosity in many students**

One of the things it takes to be a truly exceptional teacher is to be able to understand each student's needs. Just like a great coach, great teachers can somehow read each student and know when they need to be encouraged and when they need to be pushed. That's why teaching is such an art. To watch a great teacher at his or her craft is truly a pleasure.

FIVE
Forming Alliances

A very important step in helping the student overcome the underachievement syndrome is building a strong relationship between home and school. In fact, I can recall very few cases where either the home or school working independently has made a significant, positive impact on the student. To really make a change it almost always has to be a joint effort. Underachievers are masters at keeping parents and teachers apart. They realize that when the home and school unite forces it becomes much harder to divert attention away from the real problem.

The need for alliances between parents and teachers has never been greater, but somehow parents seem to have gotten the message that the schools no longer need parents' help in educating their children. I'm not exactly sure how this happened because I don't think it was intended. As our society becomes increasingly complicated and faster moving, parents and schools need to work together now more than ever. So for the record, as an unofficial representative of teachers and school personnel everywhere, let me clearly state: **We can't do it all alone! We need and want your help!**

As a parent, if your child is struggling academically, call the school today and try to set up a meeting with your child's teacher(s). In all likelihood they will be happy to hear from you. If your child is struggling, the teachers have probably been thinking about you, and have probably been thinking about giving you a call.

I'm always surprised that many parents feel like they shouldn't bother a teacher. They realize teachers are busy and don't want to take up too much of their time. A certain percentage are probably using this argument as an excuse. Truth be told, they probably do not want to bother the teacher because they don't want to be bothered themselves.

Ruling out this possibility there still remains a percentage of parents who genuinely don't feel they have sufficient reason to contact a teacher and ask for some of the teacher's time. They fail to realize how badly the teacher probably wants their help. If there is a trace of this idea in your head, wipe it out now. If a teacher genuinely feels too busy to meet with a student's parents, they are too busy. They might need to reprioritize their time.

When the time arrives for the parent/teacher meeting it's important to be clear regarding your objectives. If there is not a set agenda of what is to be accomplished, it is possible for such meetings to degenerate into what I call "the blame game." As stated, the blaming of the parents or teachers is a waste of valuable time and energy and keeps the focus away from the intent of the meeting, namely: 1) to gather and share information and 2) start formulating a multi-dimensional, multi-faceted plan to get the student back on track.

"Parent/Teacher Night" was the theme of a recent episode of "The Simpsons." A banner hung outside the school with the message "Let's Share the Blame." While the expression did strike a nerve in me, I realize now the message is fair commentary on the state of our troubled educational system. If a student isn't learning, everyone involved in the student's education is somewhat responsible...the teacher, the parents, and the student.

It is not a bad idea to have someone at this meeting to take notes. Many times excellent plans are formulated at these meetings but there is no clear understanding of who is responsible for each planned intervention. I have been at meetings where there has been a concern that the student may be having a vision or hearing problem. Someone recommends making a referral to the school nurse who is not in attendance. Everyone agrees that having a hearing and vision screening would be a good idea, but it is not clear who is responsible for contacting the school nurse. The teacher assumes the school social worker is going to contact the nurse and the social worker assumes it will be the teacher's responsibility. In the confusion the school nurse is never contacted. If someone is taking notes, the results of the meeting can be summarized before all parties leave. Copies can be made and handed out or mailed to the home. Such a form should contain the following information:

1) Student's name and grade
2) The date of the meeting
3) Who attended the meeting
4) The primary problems (only two or three)
5) Recommended interventions to correct the problem
6) Person responsible for each intervention
7) Follow up date (when the team will meet or talk again to check on the student)

Table 5.1 displays a sample copy of a form that can be used for note taking at such a meeting. It is simple, clear, only takes a few minutes and also documents that attempts are being made to meet the student's needs which is becoming increasingly important in this age of litigation. There are more parents who are suing school districts for failing to educate their children. The burden of proof is on the district to demonstrate

Table 5.1 Sample Student of Concern Form to be Used During Parent-Teacher Meeting

STUDENT OF CONCERN

Name_____ Grade_____ Date_____

Participants_____   _____

          _____   _____

          _____   _____

          _____   _____

1)Difficulty/Concern_____

_____

2)Difficulty/Concern_____

_____

3)Difficulty/Concern_____

_____

                                                    Person Responsible
1) Intervention_____(_____)

2) Intervention_____(_____)

3) Intervention_____(_____)

Date of Follow-Up-Meeting_____Time_____Location_____

that there were attempts made to make adjustments for the student. A form like this may keep your district out of a law suit or save the day if there ever is one. This is a form that can be modified in any number of ways to include other information that is of interest.

An important decision to be made is whether or not the student should attend such a meeting. There are two schools of thought on this question.

Some believe that since it is the student who is the concern, it is senseless to hold a meeting to discuss plans for the student unless they are in attendance and are actively involved in the decision making. Others will argue that with the student in attendance teachers will be less than 100% honest, not wanting to hurt the student's feelings. Additionally, having students listen to teacher(s) describe their less-than-stellar performance can be damaging to the child's self-confidence. I must admit that I have been at meetings where the teachers take turns explaining how poorly the student is performing and, as they go around the table, the student becomes more and more distressed. Is this necessarily a bad thing? I don't think so. It needs to be made clear to the student that the intent of the meeting is to help them perform more effectively. The student may feel picked on but hopefully a sense that teachers are concerned about his or her progress will come through.

My solution involves a compromise: during the initial portions of the meeting it might be best not to have the student in attendance . It is true that some teachers, out of compassion, tend to minimize a problem, not wanting to hurt the child's feelings. If having the student in the room during the problem identification portion of the meeting will cause teachers to be anything less than totally forthcoming then the student should not be in attendance.

Once the information regarding the student's behavior and grades has been discussed and it's time to start formulating a plan, the student could be invited into the meeting. When I am at a meeting like this and the student enters the room I usually tell them, "Now we really need your help. You know we're here because things at school haven't been going as well as they could be. It's time to get back on the right track so we're going to work on a plan to help you get going again. We all want you to feel that this plan is fair because you have to be able to live with it. That's why we need you to help us out." A behavioral contract will be discussed later but be very clear about one thing: **If a student doesn't feel a plan is fair, the interventions are probably not going to work.** What seems fair to adults may seem totally unfair to a student. Also, by inviting the student to have input in the plan they gain a sense of ownership. Think for a minute about your own life, whether it be work, home, or anywhere. Do you like being told what's going to happen to you? Of course not. Most individuals initial reaction is to resist and, subsequently, dig their heels in even deeper. Students are the same way and why shouldn't they be? No one likes feeling controlled.

An important point for parents to deal with before they attend a conference is that they are probably going to feel uncomfortable. The teachers are going to tell you things about your son or daughter that will be hard to sit and listen to. Expect this and, in the best way you can, prepare yourself. After all, you are having this meeting because there is a problem. Hopefully, teachers will be kind and tactful. Be warned, however, that if you feel frustrated with your child's performance, his or her teachers are probably also frustrated. Having warned you let me now reassure you.

An overwhelming majority of these meetings are very successful. If nothing else such a meeting demonstrates to your child that you are concerned and willing to put forth time and energy regarding his or her education.

It may be helpful to prepare a list of questions to remind yourself of the points you want to cover. Diane Heacox (1991) suggests the following questions:

1) What seems to be the cause of my child's grade in math? reading ? etc.
2) Does my child have the capability to be in this class?
3) Does he/she ask for help in class?

4) Does he/she appear to be paying attention in class?
5) Are there circumstances in the class that may be distracting him/her? (For example, does my child sit next to a best friend?)
6) Does he/she participate in class discussion?
7) Is his/her work turned in on time?
8) Does my child follow directions?
9) Do students in your class have time in class to work on homework?
10) What are the standards for grades?

This list is an excellent start but I think there are a few that need to be included.

11) Is the problem with test scores, daily assignments, or both?
12) Is my child missing assignments that could still be turned in to receive credit?
13) How many days has my child been absent or tardy?

The last question is important to make certain that your child is actually going to school. I've been at numerous meetings where a parent learns that a student has been marked absent eight times during first period. The parent knows that the student is leaving the house every morning at 7:15 A.M. but did not realize the student was not always making it to school.

Another example of the ingenuity that underachievers can display is perfectly illustrated by Kurt, a fourth grade student. In a similar circumstance, Kurt was being reported tardy to school on numerous occasions. He walked to school and would simply take his time getting there so he would not have to sit through the first subject of the day, math, which he disliked. After meeting with the father, who was concerned and willing to do whatever necessary, a plan was formulated that would have the father drive Kurt to school each morning. Everyone left the meeting feeling very confident that the problem of tardiness was dealt with in a satisfactory manner. After all, with his father dropping him off at the front door, how could Kurt keep missing math? Somehow the problem continued as two or three times a week Kurt would wander into class about forty minutes late. School personnel assumed that the father, for some reason, was not able to drive Kurt to school each day and, therefore, he was showing up late on the days he walked. It was almost by accident that the school found out what Kurt was doing.

Kurt's father was driving him to school each and every morning. I was at school for an early meeting one day and saw Kurt come into the building ten minutes early. When I saw his teacher later that day I commented that at least Kurt was on time today. The teacher explained that he was late coming to class that day as well. With some minor detective work the next day, we found out how Kurt had been keeping up this tardiness game. Kurt had been hiding in the last stall in the bathroom during first period math! He wouldn't do it every morning because he was smart enough to realize that missing each morning would probably mean a phone call to his father. He knew once the school and parent communicated they would realize something was wrong...all this from a fourth grader!

Reports Home

In order to keep the communication between home and school ongoing, I highly recommend some type of routine report home. It can't be overemphasized that when school and parents keep in close contact, many of the avenues that students use to avoid being held accountable simply no longer work. The proverbial oldest trick in the book (i.e. "I did all my work at school") will no longer be a possibility. Also eliminated is the game of misleading parents about the requirements for a project. The student's tendency to "forget" about the spelling test will no longer be a problem because such information will be communicated through the reports home. Reports home are a headache and they do require extra work for both parents and teachers but they're worth the effort. They allow for the parents to keep abreast of the child's progress and provide the school with access to the parents. As I've said to parents before, "You control most of the good stuff like allowances, privileges, car keys, and curfews. If we can make the 'good stuff' dependent on school work, we have a much better chance of changing the student's behavior."

Other advantages of reports coming home are described by Kelley (1990):

1) Reports home require parents and teachers to jointly define behaviors they want to focus on changing. This collaboration focuses on solving problems rather than assigning blame.

2) Reports home require parents and teachers to work together so that neither party is solely responsible for solving the problems.

3) Notes home provide parents with frequent information on the student's progress.

4) Reports home focus on positive rather than negative behavior. Students are, therefore, more likely to receive increased parental praise and attention.

5) Students often appreciate and respond to the added information regarding their performance.

6) Parents are responsible for administering the consequences (the "good stuff" and "bad stuff") and the amount of time required from a teacher is minimal.

7) Teachers are not asked to alter their teaching style or instructional techniques and are thus more likely to view the notes home as an acceptable intervention.

8) Since reinforcers are typically provided at the end of the day, students are gaining experience delaying gratification and tolerating frustration.

How often do these reports need to be sent home? With elementary school aged students, I recommend daily reports. The biggest reason for daily reports is not necessarily academic. Younger students have a different frame of reference with regard to time than do older students. To a first grader, the idea that if they don't do their spelling on Monday they won't get to sleep over at a friend's house on Friday may not matter. Waiting until the end of the week for a special prize is too long. The idea that if they don't do their spelling today, they won't be allowed to watch television after school has much more of an impact. With younger students, whenever possible, make the rewards and consequences as immediate as possible.

Obviously, each child is different but when in doubt, start with daily reports. If in a few weeks your system is working you can always lessen the frequency of the reports home. After a while you can use a Monday-Wednesday-Friday schedule and eventually just a weekly note home on Friday should suffice.

These reports can take many forms and do not have to be elaborate. With early elementary students, they can be as simple as a happy face for a good day and a frowning face for a bad day. It is usually a good idea to include an area for "comments" so that the parent and teacher can communicate back and forth regarding the student's progress. Following is a sample of several forms that may give you some ideas for use with your student. The first form (Table 5.2) is designed for a student who has numerous teachers such as a middle schooler. The second form (Table 5.3) includes information regarding the student's percentage of correctly completed work. The third form (Table 5.4) has an emphasis on cooperation with the teacher. Feel free to modify these forms in any way that would more appropriately serve your needs.

During the first few days of reports, if at all possible, give the student the benefit of the doubt. By that I mean that if, as a teacher, you are faced with a borderline day, try to allow the student to take home a good report so that they can receive the reward. By borderline day I mean the type of day that the student has not done a great job on every task but has done at least satisfactory work. Never give the student a good report if they have clearly had a bad day. To do so would only reinforce the student's inappropriate behavior.

There's an old saying that "nothing succeeds like success." A little reward and praise can encourage a child to work hard the next day and the next and soon there is a snowball effect. You might have a child who perhaps for the first time in her life is starting to think she has real capabilities as a student. It may be the first time school has been a successful experience.

If the student is mature enough, he/she can record the assignments. The teacher then merely has to initial in the appropriate location or sign the bottom of the form which indicates the assignments recorded are correct. If needed there can be modifications to make certain assignments are turned into the teacher. The report home is also an excellent reminder regarding which books need to be taken home. The student simply needs to look at the assignment list and figure out which classes have assignments that are not finished.

Notice the inconvenience to the teacher in this scenario is minimal. The teacher simply has to make sure the assignments are correct and sign his or her name. This would require a total time commitment of less than ten seconds.

At the parent meeting, it's helpful to get the times when a teacher is available for phone calls. There will occasionally be instances that arise when the parent may want to talk to the teacher regarding a missing assignment or some other circumstance. I can only speak for myself when I say I don't mind being called at home occasionally, but try not to call unless it is an emergency. The problem arises in that some parents may tend to view ALL situations as emergencies. Please ask your child's teacher(s) about availability for home calls and if so, appropriate times.

The Carrot and The Stick

Sometimes parents believe that they can make their child perform better in school. They think that because they are adults they will simply make their child perform more effectively. They haven't thought about *how* but, "By God, no child of mine is going to get an F." This typically means taking away privileges, giving lectures, making threats, and other methods that are usually ineffective. I'm not saying you have to sit by and watch your child fail. There are obviously many things that can be done which have been discussed so far throughout this book. The point I'm trying to reemphasize is this: you can't make children do something they really don't want to do.

Table 5.2 Sample of a Daily Assignment Sheet

DAILY ASSIGNMENT SHEET

NAME_____ DATE_____
SUBJECT
Mathematics_____ Teachers Initials_____
Due Date_____
Comments_____

Reading_____ Teachers Initials_____
Due Date_____
Comments_____

Social Studies_____ Teachers Initials_____
Due Date_____
Comments_____

Science_____ Teachers Initials_____
Due Date_____
Comments_____

Computers_____ Teachers Initials_____
Due Date_____
Comments_____

Art/Band_____ Teachers Initials_____
Due Date_____
Comments_____

Parent's Signature_____
Comments_____
_____
_____

Table 5.3 Sample Note Home with Emphasis on Percentage of Work Completed Correctly

REPORT TO PARENTS

NAME_____   DATE_____

SUBJECT
Math
Assignment Handed In YES_____ NO_____
% of homework completed correctly _____
Comments_____

Reading
Assignment Handed In YES_____ NO_____
% of homework completed correctly _____
Comments_____

Spelling
Assignment Handed In YES_____ NO_____
% of homework completed correctly _____
Comments_____

Social Studies
Assignment Handed In YES_____ NO_____
% of homework completed correctly _____
Comments_____

Science
Assignment Handed In YES_____ NO_____
% of homework completed correctly _____
Comments_____

English
Assignment Handed In YES_____ NO_____
% of homework completed correctly _____
Cooments_____

Parent's Signature_____
Comments_____
_____
_____

Table 5.4 Sample of a Report Home with an Emphasis on Behavior

REPORT TO PARENTS

NAME_____   DATE_____

SUBJECT
Math
Student followed classroom rules: excellent   average   unacceptable

Student earned the following grade for his/her behavior in my class today:
       A   B   C   D   F
Comments_____Initials_____

Science
Student followed classroom rules: excellent   average   unacceptable

Student earned the following grade for his/her behavior in my class today:
       A   B   C   D   F
Comments_____Initials_____

Social Studies
Student followed classroom rules: excellent   average   unacceptable

Student earned the following grade for his/her behavior in my class today:
       A   B   C   D   F
Comments_____Initials_____

English
Student followed classroom rules: excellent   average   unacceptable

Student earned the following grade for his/her behavior in my class today:
       A   B   C   D   F
Comments_____Initials_____

Band
Student followed classroom rules: excellent   average   unacceptable

Student earned the following grade for his/her behavior in my class today:
       A   B   C   D   F
Comments_____Initials_____
Parents Signature_____
Comments_____

It simply can't be done. If students absolutely and totally resist the change, you can not place the knowledge in their head and make it come out through their pencil.

All that really can be done is set up very specific expectations for their behavior and hold them strictly accountable for their choices. If they choose not to abide by the rules, they are choosing to suffer the consequences. If they choose to live up to these expectations, they are choosing to reap the rewards. In short, they can either work toward something or work to avoid something…the **carrot** or the **stick.** They either reach for the carrot or work to avoid the stick.

Another reason not to get into an absolute battle of wills with your children has nothing to do with the fact that you can not control them. An even better reason not to get into an all out power struggle is that you'll lose. Not only will you lose but you'll lose badly and you'll lose almost every time you decide to battle. Why? Because you love them. You love them very much and they know this. Armed with that knowledge they can crush your heart to the finest powder. Trust me when I say the key is to negotiate. That doesn't mean give in and give up. It means if both can live with a plan there will be more peace and everybody will be happier.

I've included a couple of sample contracts to give you a starting point if you decide to try this approach with your student. Table 5.5 is an example of the type of contract I like to use with high school students. It is intentionally written with a lot of legal sounding language because I've found that students seem to like this type of verbiage. Somehow it makes this behavioral contract seem more like a "real" contract. The contract presented in Table 5.6 is an example of a contract you might use with an elementary student.

Another important point when setting up a contract is to focus on reinforcement, not punishment. Research has consistently shown that rewards work better than punishment. There seems to be a pattern in America that we punish, punish, punish and fail to consider the fact that there are other alternatives. I hear stories every week from parents who say they've grounded the child, taken away this, taken away that and nothing works. I always say "Would your son do his Algebra if, for example, he'd get a new car if he finished?" Parents always say, "Of course he would" to which I reply, "Then there is something he'll work toward. Now we just need to find out what that is and make sure you folks can live with it." When parents say "Nothing works" what they are really saying is "Nothing we've tried has worked." Everyone (including your students) has something they'll work toward.

Another reason to focus on rewards rather than punishment is that it will probably improve the mood around the dinner table. If the only conversation you seem to have with your intelligent 16-year-old is telling him what he can't have or can't do on Saturday, you're probably not going to be nominated for "parent of the year." It's a lot more fun for you and your child to hand out reinforcers.

Once you've found something your child is willing to work toward there is another problem that will arise in time. For example, let's say you work out a plan with your twelve-year-old son which would allow him to go roller skating on Friday night if all his homework is completed. He's thrilled with this idea and on Friday brings home his weekly report from school with nothing but completed work. There are several comments from his teachers, "Mike had a great week. Keep up the good work!," "Not only did Michael complete his work but his test scores were up, too!"

You are thrilled and verbally praise Michael, "I'm so proud of you. Look what a little extra effort can do. You did such a good job I'm going to give you an extra dollar for treats at the roller rink." Michael goes roller skating and has fun, God is back in heaven, and all the headaches over grades, assignments, and tests seem to be a thing of the past.

Next Friday comes and the reports come home and again, all the assignments have been completed. You notice however there's only one comment this time and it's not exactly a positive one, "Michael's money for the field trip needs to be in no later than Monday." Oh well, all the assignments are completed and that's what counts. Michael again gets to go roller skating but instead of coming in at 10:30 P.M. (which is his curfew) he walks in the door at 9:45 P.M. You ask if he had a good time to which he replies, "Yeah, I guess."

The following week when the report comes from Michael's teachers he has two missing math assignments and a missed book report. The contract specifically states that Michael will not be allowed to go skating if there is any incomplete work. You brace for a confrontation expecting Michael to be upset and put up a fight when he's told he can't go skating. You're surprised and somewhat confused when you tell him he can't go skating and he shrugs and asks, "What's for dinner?"

What's going on here? What happened to the perfect little plan that seemed to be working so well?

The problem here is that Michael has become tired of the reward. The first week of skating was great because he hadn't been skating for three months. A week later it was all right, but he had just been roller skating. In the third week, the thought of skating didn't appeal that much and it certainly wasn't worth two math assignments and a book report on *The Red Badge of Courage*. Roller skating was getting old...fast!

To overcome this problem you have to shift the reward. What I always recommend is that you and your child have a list of reinforcers that the child is allowed to pick from. Within a month Michael will probably be willing to work very hard to earn another roller skating trip. He just wasn't excited about it for the third week in a row. Now, if Mom and Dad had only known that a great movie was just out at the video store and that Michael would have given anything (even a book report!) to see it, things might have been different. So generate a list and the more options you can come up with the better. During the week you can ask, "What are you working for this week? Are you caught up?" Once you know he's wanting to get his own frozen pizza for Friday night you can remind him of that as a motivator.

The following is a list of a few rewards I have had students work toward. These are just ideas that may or may not be applicable to your child. Remember, you know your child better than anyone.

-phone privileges	-video rental
-curfew extensions	-use of car
-pizza	-soft drink
-reduced chores	-later bedtime
-candy	-a special toy
-Nintendo rental	-special trip
-camping	-friend staying over
-cassette tape	-privilege to wear make-up
-special meal	-going to the movies
-special time with parents	-playing outside
-new t-shirt	-not having to baby-sit
-money	-bed not being made

Sample Programs

Following is a selection of different programs that are recommended for students at various ages. These ideas are presented with numerous options to be decided regarding your comfort level and child's preference.

A child who is underachieving may be struggling for any number of reasons. One of the possibilities is that the child may be having difficulties due to genuine learning problems. In a later chapter there will be a detailed discussion of the evaluation process.

Let's assume for the time being that the student does not have significant processing deficits or learning difficulties. Let's assume the difficulties are primarily related to the issues that have been previously discussed such as manipulation, low frustration tolerance, and disorganization.

The first step, meeting with the teacher, has already been discussed. When this appointment is being arranged you may want to inquire as to the possibility of some of the school specialists also attending the meeting. In most districts there are school psychologists, schools social workers, remedial reading and math teachers, learning disabilities specialists and/or emotional disabilities specialists. Let me briefly de-

Table 5.5 Sample Behavioral Contract for Middle School/High School Student

Contract

The following contract is voluntarily entered into by all parties involved. The terms of this contract shall continue as stated below until all parties are in agreement as to the modifications to be made. This contract is terminated only when all parties agree that the contract is null and void.

Bill Smith, from here on referred to as "the Student", and Dick and Jane Smith, from here on referred to as "the Parents," do hereby agree to the following terms:

1) That the student will bring home all daily assignment sheets
2) That the parents will review all daily assignment sheets
3) All assignments must be completed and turned in on time for the week
4) Any missed assignments will result in a suspension of weekend privileges until said assignments are completed by the Student and examined by the Parents
5) If all assignments are completed, turned in on time, and all daily notes are brought home, the student will be allowed to select from the following list of reinforcers:

    -extended curfew until 1:00 a.m.

    -video rental

    -Parents pay for movie and treat

    -use of the car either Friday or Saturday evening

    -No chores for the weekend, specifically-no dishes or garbage removal

The undersigned agree to the terms of this contract and signify this agreement by signing below.

_____   _____   _____

Bill Smith   Dick Smith   Jane Smith

Date_____

Table 5.6 Sample Contract for an Elementary School Student

Contract

Mom and Dad will allow Steve to go to the roller skating rink on Friday night if he brings home four of five "Happy Notes" from Mrs. Jeffries. Steve can also earn extra privileges if he has a perfect week and brings home five "Happy Notes." Steve can choose one of the follwing special rewards for having a perfect week.

1) Rides his bike to a friends house on Saturday

2) Gets to stay up until 9:00 p.m. on Friday night

3) Gets to choose his favorite meal for lunch on either Saturday of Sunday

4) Gets to go to Hardees for lunch

_____   _____
Steve   Mom and Dad
Date_____

scribe the various roles these individuals fill within the schools. The descriptions may not be totally accurate because professionals may have their roles defined differently at each district. For example, as a school psychologist I have worked in districts where I did a great deal of ongoing counseling and other districts where I did virtually no counseling. I have worked in districts where I have been relied upon to help teachers with difficult children (like underachievers) and districts where my primary responsibility has been completing diagnostic evaluations. The same type of variance across different districts is probably true for each of the following professionals. However, all of these individuals will have expertise and may be able to add significantly to the meeting no matter what their roles may be within their district.

School Psychologist

The psychologist typically is in charge of diagnostic evaluations for children who are referred to determine whether they qualify for special educational services such as learning disabled, emotionally disturbed, or mentally handicapped. These professionals have specialized training in educational/psychological assessment, counseling, behavior modification, and consultation.

School Social Worker

Most school social workers are primarily involved with the responsibility of being a liaison between home and school with families whose children are struggling academically, behaviorally, and/or emotionally. Many also are heavily involved in running student support groups and individual counseling.

Reading Specialist/Chapter 1 Reading

There are some districts where these positions are separate in that the district has both a reading specialist and a Chapter 1 reading teacher. Many smaller districts combine these positions. Chapter 1 reading is a federally funded program that provides small group instruction for students who fall at or below the thirty-third percentile in reading according to their scores on their spring achievement tests.

Chapter 1 Math

The above description can also be applied to Chapter 1 math.

Learning Disabilities Specialist

These teachers instruct children who have been diagnosed with a learning disability. They have specialized training in understanding how children learn and in the remediation of academic deficits.

Emotional and/or Behavioral Disabilities Specialists

These teachers work with students who qualify for small group programming due to emotional or behavioral difficulties. They have specialized skills in behavior modification and many times are excellent additions to the "team" because they use contracts and reinforcers with many of their students.

I describe these individuals at this point because often the school may want some of them at the initial meeting. You may hear terms such as "child study team" or "student of concern committee" and these groups are typically made up of these professionals.

It may be your preference to hold the initial meeting with just the classroom teacher. In that case the meeting tends to be less formal and it can be easier to simply discuss some ideas the teacher may have to help get the child motivated and back on the right track academically. The choice regarding the nature of the meeting and who should attend should really be up to the parents. If the parents do not want to meet with four or five professionals they can request a meeting with just their child's teacher.

Sometimes there can be too much help. One of the districts I used to work at had eight or nine specialists at each meeting. All of these highly trained professionals had input on each child and the meetings became much longer than was necessary. For that reason I prefer a team of no more than five or six members.

At this meeting the teacher or other school personnel may have a plan to try with your child because they have had success with a student who was having similar difficulties. If that is the case and the plan makes sense, you might want to give it a try. However, objections or concerns had better be voiced. Remember, even though all the individuals at these meetings are experts, you are an expert in the most important area...YOUR CHILD. No one at that meeting knows your child better than you do.

Here is an example of a structured plan that I typically start with. Modification will probably be needed, as each situation is unique. It is then important to realize that this model is very adaptable to numerous situations with a host of different difficulties.

Early Elementary
Step 1—Daily Notes Home

Daily notes home are virtually a must at these grade levels. This period of a child's academic career is extremely important. It is at the early elementary level that children establish their work patterns, opinions regarding school, ability to tolerate frustration, and numerous other important factors. With daily notes home the parent has immediate feedback regarding the child's progress. Why wait a week to determine if things are going satisfactorily? In a week's time the child could miss out on an important skill.

Another important consideration has to do with what constitutes a good versus bad day. With a kindergartner, a good day may be when they performed a majority of tasks throughout the day without complaining or resisting. It is important to keep in mind whether or not the expectations for your son or daughter are similar to the expectations for the rest of the class. In most cases, the classroom teacher can be responsible for determining a good day from a bad day. If the student also has expectations regarding his behavior on the bus and at lunch, then other individuals may have to be consulted before a judgment can be made.

Your initial plan may be very simple in that the only modification needed for incomplete assignments would be to work during recess until the assignment is complete. Often one half of a missed recess causes the student to be more motivated. I recommend the child only has to stay in from recess until the assignment is completed. If the assignment consists of ten problems and the student has seven completed, it should only take them a couple of minutes to finish the last three. The goal is to get the assignment completed and once that is done, let them enjoy their recess period. Staying in from recess, even if for a short time, still gives the student a clear message that incomplete work is not acceptable.

Whenever possible, keep the plans simple. Teachers have a million things to keep track of during the day and don't want to have an elaborate system to follow as well. If a simple system will take care of the problem, then follow that plan. An important portion of the plan is making the expectations clear to the student. This is the most commonly overlooked portion of the plan and the reason many plans fail. I recommend expectations for the student be put in writing at the meeting. At a later time both the parents and teacher can go over the expectations with the student.

We tend to assume students know exactly what is appropriate and what is not but this is often not the case. General statements such as "acting like a good boy" or "following the rules" leave too much in doubt. Spell out exactly the rules that are to be followed:

1) Will complete and hand in all required assignments.

2) Will bring a note home to his mother and father every day.

3) Will return the note to the teacher the next morning.

4) Will raise his hand to ask for help when needed.

With younger elementary children it may be a good idea to break the day in half so that it is possible for the student to earn two rewards. The agreement can be that if the student completes all class work during the morning they receive a smiling face or sticker. If they have a successful afternoon, they can receive a reward for the afternoon as well.

There are several advantages to dividing the day into two parts. If the student has a really bad morning they can always earn credit for the afternoon. They can still be motivated to try and salvage one sticker for the day. There have been times when the child knows by 10:00 A.M. that they can not receive a good report home. At this point they have no reason to control their behavior and seem to feel free to do whatever they please for the rest of the afternoon.

Children at this age have very short attention spans. Breaking the day into two parts shortens the amount of time they have to wait to receive a reward. To children, it seems easier to behave appropriately until lunch time or first recess. Behaving until the end of the day seems much too long.

A word to the wise to teachers but especially parents... don't underestimate the power of the almighty sticker! Children at this age will do almost anything for a sticker. It is a sad day indeed when "sticker magic" wears off. It becomes harder to motivate students. More time, energy, and planning has to be put into the selection of reinforcers when this happens. Stickers are also nice because they can be displayed at home on the refrigerator for a job well done.

Some programs are dual edged in that if the child acts appropriately, they receive a reward but if they fail to act appropriately, they receive punishment or negative reinforcement. Punishment and negative reinforcement are commonly confused. Punishment is the administration of an unpleasant stimulus such as giving the child a spanking. Negative reinforcement is the deliberate withholding of a reward such as taking away the Nintendo.

As an example, Polly, a fourth grader, was struggling in school. She was well liked by her peers and generally appeared to be a well adjusted child but there had always been concerns about her academic progress. It took her longer to catch on to concepts and she had to work harder to keep up with her classmates.

It's unclear exactly what brought things to a head in fourth grade but Polly had a difficult first quarter. It could have been due to the complexity of the school work or it might have been a result of Polly's increasing resentment toward her parents. They were actively involved with her academically and, as always, attended parent/teacher conferences that fall. They were told by Mr. Showalter, her teacher, that Polly had not been turning in all her assignments. She also had not been keeping her parents informed regarding school events.

Upon learning that she had been letting her school work slide, her parents immediately disciplined Polly by taking away her roller blades which she received over the summer. They were certain that things would start improving but when they heard from Mr. Showalter things had not changed. The parents decided to make Polly go to bed by 7:00 P.M. until her work improved but that did not seem to help either. Next they made Polly come straight home from school instead of allowing her to participate in soccer. There was still no change in her performance.

When I met with the parents they explained what had been done prior to our meeting to motivate Polly. It became clear that the emphasis of their plan was entirely on the negative and did not touch upon the positive. All the focus was on punishment or negative reinforcement and there was no opportunity to earn rewards. Instead of focusing on punishing Polly, I recommended they allow her to earn back her privileges. If she could bring home three positive daily notes the following week, I suggested they allow her to play soccer. If she could bring home four of five positive notes the week after that, she could resume her Rollerblading or be returned to her previous bed time.

As I suspected, Polly was motivated to earn back her privileges and her school work began to get better. She told me later that she wasn't going to "let them blackmail me!" For some reason, she viewed working toward those privileges as fair but taking them away as unfair.

My reasons for encouraging the use of rewards rather than negative reinforcers has nothing to do with how I feel ethically about punishment and negative reinforcement. I recommend the use of rewards for the simple reason that they work better than punishments.

Upper Elementary–Middle School

One of the biggest differences between lower elementary students and this age group is that the reinforcers these students are willing to work toward are different. The stickers have usually lost their charm by this point. Now we have to be more creative.

In middle school, the student will have multiple teachers which often complicates things. When a student is in one classroom for an entire day it is obviously much easier for a teacher to be consistent. They can be more sensitive to the needs of the student because they control the classroom environment. When a teacher only has contact with a student for 45-52 minutes per day much of that consistency is lost. Also the teacher loses the sense of responsibility for the student's performance. Instead of feeling responsible for the student in his or her entirety, each teacher feels responsible for only one subject area.

If you are still using daily notes, the student will probably have to be responsible for getting the notes from teacher to teacher in the various classes. With the disorganization of many underachievers, this can be a significant problem. The other way to view this situation is that these students need to learn to be responsible just like everyone else. Getting a daily note to teachers and then getting the note home is an important part of the plan. If they are to receive credit for a good days work, this is a portion of what is involved in receiving that credit.

The notes will change as well. Smiley faces and "Billy had a good day" will no longer be sufficient. I recommend having a teacher circle either "satisfactory" or "unsatisfactory" next to the subject area. If the student has homework the teacher should sign or initial next to the homework signifying the homework the student has recorded on the assignment sheet is correct.

Weekly Notes

By upper elementary and middle school it is common to use weekly notes. The obvious choice is Friday for the "day of truth."

There are two basic choices for weekly notes. The child can have a note that records the assignments for each day of the week. The note is kept at school and is the total responsibility of the student. A problem can arise in that the note gets lost or basically disintegrates from all the handling during the week. It has the advantage of serving as a type of assignment log. The student always has a list of what assignments were given out during that week. As the assignments get handed in they can be checked off the list.

The other choice is the type of note that the student distributes to each teacher on Friday. The teachers either states something to the effect that "all assignments were handed in" or "two assignments missing. Page 14, problems 1–10. Page 16, 12–20."

If the student brings home a note that states, "All assignments complete" they should receive the agreed upon reward. If they bring home a note that indicates that they've missed assignments, all privileges should be suspended until these assignments are completed. That means no phone, no friends over, and no anything until these assignments are completed. The missing assignments can usually be finished by Friday evening and the student has the rest of the weekend to relax and have fun. Some parents will allow the student to have Friday night off and start work on Saturday. The logic here being that the student has been in school all week and will do better work if they are allowed a night off. Parents should use their own judgment here but be aware that when you give an inch, these students may want a mile. The following example shows how this situation can backfire.

You decide to let your student take Friday night off

because he's only missing two assignments. You stand firm, however, that he is not granted Friday night privileges because the agreement was clear: Any missing assignments will not be tolerated and will result in a suspension of normal privileges until those assignments are completed. As the clock approaches 7:00 P.M., your son says, "Mom, Dad...couldn't I go to the basketball game just this once. I'm not going to start work on my homework until tomorrow anyway." You've already given ground and now he's asking for more. If you agree and let him go, you have only reinforced his hunch that there was the possibility of a cave-in to this plan. If you forbid the privilege there will probably be an angry confrontation. Now you have a battle that you didn't bargain for when the contract was agreed upon.

Once again, you know your child better than anyone but be forewarned that these situations will arise. It might be better to get the child to sit down and complete the assignments so he can go to the game just like everyone else.

Trouble Shooting

I can virtually promise you that the student will "test the limits" with this new program. Don't be surprised if the first week there are numerous assignments not completed. The student is determining whether or not you are serious and are going to follow through on your promises. "Will they really make me stay at home all weekend if I have missing assignments?" the student is asking. Well, will you? Be very honest with yourself now because it is much worse to start a program like this only to give in a week or so later. The child gets the message that , "My parents won't really follow through. I can wait them out and call their bluff." It would be better to do nothing than to start a program like this and give up after a week.

The most common tactic is for students to "accidentally" lose their notes on the way home. Failing to bring home a note should be treated as a failure to keep their end of the bargain. It needs to be clearly spelled out in the contract that one phase of successful fulfillment of the agreement is getting the notes home. A lost note is like no note at all. If the student insists the assignments were completed there is always one way to make certain. Call the teacher and ask if all the assignments have been turned in during the week. Usually you only have to do this one time because after calling their bluff once they typically won't try to fool you again.

For this program to have any chance of working the parents have to stick to the letter of the law of the contract. Will the student fight you? Perhaps. Will they try and trick you? Possibly. Will this program work if you stick to it? Probably. Once the student realizes you are serious and he or she will spend the entire weekend sitting at the kitchen table completing assignments they may have major motivation to do these assignments at school. I've seen it take three or four long weekends for the student and parents, but I've also seen this same child on the honor role a few weeks later. The student needs to realize the parents are dead serious and past behavior patterns will not be tolerated. This is what I like to think of as **"light vs. heat."** You can't always make them see the light (i.e. that their school work is important) but you can make them feel the heat!

Homework Time

I believe it is a good idea to set up a specific time for homework each night, for example, from 7:00 P.M. to 7:45 P.M. That means the television is shut off and the only activity for that forty-five minutes is homework.

There is room within this approach for flexibility. If a unique situation arises that is taking place at the same time as the homework time, it is perfectly acceptable to move up the homework time to allow the student to free up their normal homework time slot.

The student should have a "homework area" that is conducive to work. There should be a minimum of distractions and adequate space and light. I do not recommend that the homework is done while lying in bed with the new Guns 'N' Roses tape playing in the background. Hopefully, there is an area that is already adequate for homework or one can be arranged.

If your son, for example, says, "I've got no homework" I initially would remind him of the terms of the contract. If he does have homework, you're going to know about it on Friday so he might as well work on it now as opposed to over the weekend. If he still maintains he has no homework it is a good idea to use that time to work on some of his weaker skills. Many underachievers are at grade level in certain subjects but almost all students have an area or areas where they could use some catching up. At some point these deficits will have to be overcome. Why not use this time slot?

I don't, however, think it is a good idea for a student to spend hour after hour plugging away at homework except when backed up with late work. When getting caught up it may take a few hard evenings of work. On a nightly basis I don't think it's wise to spend two to three hours (or more) doing homework. For one thing, your household will probably not bear the strain that will arise from marathon homework. I've seen parents get really involved and overly "fired up" about getting a child back on track. They attack the problem with a vengeance and are convinced that all the student's problems will be solved in a couple of weeks. What usually happens is that everyone gets worn out. It's better to have a program that stipulates a set amount of time for homework each evening. If the student honestly is working during that time he or she will probably be able to finish the assignments anyway. It's important to remember that this problem didn't happen overnight and it won't go away over night.

To Tutor or Not To Tutor

If you are the parent or teacher of a child who is struggling academically, you've got a basic decision to make….how involved do I get with the school work in trying to help?

As a psychologist who works with families of under-achieving children, I see many instances where a family really wants to break the cycle of failure. The problem is that they spend a lot of time and energy very inefficiently. Many times they simply start trying to help before they really understand the problem.

There are many, many reasons children do not perform well academically. The student may have legitimate learning problems that are interfering with his or her ability to read, write, and do arithmetic. The student may be emotionally troubled. The student may be doing his or her best and still be struggling due to low ability, alcohol or drug problems, low motivation, health factors, etc. This list could go on for several pages but the important point is…**Before we can start focusing on how we can change a pattern of failure into a pattern of success we had better make certain there is a clear understanding of the reasons for failure in the first place.** For now let's refocus on the commitment you can make as a parent or teacher to help the student.

To some parents the idea of functioning as a personal tutor to their child is a natural extension of parental responsibilities. They were probably raised in homes where parents spent a portion of most nights at the kitchen table helping with math problems, quizzed children for spelling tests, and proofreading English assignments. These types of activities were no different than changing the babies diapers or teaching their child to ride a bike.

For other parents, tutoring is something viewed as the job of the school or other individuals. The idea of working as a surrogate teacher is not something they view as part of their job as parents.

Before I go on I want to assure you that these two descriptions are not intended to sound pejorative. Some of you were probably waiting for me to make the broad overgeneralization that, "Parents who are willing to be tutors are good. Non-tutoring parents are bad." It's just not that simple.

My parents raised five children. Since we all went to thirteen years of public education that's sixty-five years of schooling. I'm not certain but I don't think any of my brothers or sisters missed the honor roll more than once or twice. I can count on one hand the number of times I recall my parents actually directly helping me with homework. I do remember having some difficulties with long division and my father showing me a technique to keep the steps straight. We all did well in school but not because my parents spent a lot of time tutoring us.

What they did do was set very clear expectations that we **were** going to do well academically. If we slipped up and brought home a poor report card or a failure notice, there would have been some very real consequences. We never questioned that.

What I'd like you to ask yourself if you're considering tutoring your child is, "Do I have the time and energy to stick with this?" It does take time and it's not something you can do only when you feel like it. Remember, a science test will still be on Thursday even if you've had a really rough day at the office on Wednesday. If tutoring is not something you feel up to handling on a regular basis, it is best to set up other plans from the very beginning.

One thing to consider when you are deciding whether or not you are going to become involved as an active tutor is can I afford to hire a professional tutor? Tutors are available in nearly every town or city, but they can become quite expensive. As with anything, the better the tutor, the more expensive they will be. If you are the parent of an elementary school child, could a high school student do an adequate job of tutoring? This might be a great solution to your problem. To a fourth or fifth grader, high school students are looked up to and having a sixteen-year-old come to your house to work with the student may make homework more enjoyable. The student may even work harder to please the tutor.

Also, most high school students will think that helping a student with math for $5.00 an hour is a pretty easy way to make money. I suggest calling the school and asking for the names of students who might be willing to tutor a few hours a week. They usually can give you three or four names of kids they think would be good tutors. Also, the guidance department can be a good source of students. There are even organizations like the National Honor Society or Future

Teachers of America that have to do community service projects and are looking for ways to help.

If your child is high school age, try using the same basic approach with the local college. Those of you who went to college will probably remember how tight money was and most departments keep a list of students willing to do tutoring. You'll have to pay a little more, but it may be well worth it.

I've also come across situations where students pursuing advanced degrees have projects where they have to spend time working one-on-one with students teaching reading skills, for example. I recall spending many hours with a third grader struggling with numerous academic subjects as part of a project in a class on behavior modification. It costs the parents absolutely nothing, the child received some intense one-on-one help, and I completed my project. Everyone came out ahead.

Another avenue to explore is asking if there are structured tutorial times at school. Many schools have programs that students can attend during their study halls to receive extra help. Often times there are resources available right in the school that are not being used that are free. Some schools have programs such as homework hotlines that set up specific times to call after school where their questions can be answered by a tutor.

Don't forget about teachers! I'm continually amazed at how many times teachers volunteer their time to help if the student is willing to come to them. Teachers may be at school early or have some time after lunch during which they would be happy to help. What parents often forget is that teachers want to see your child succeed almost as badly as you do. They teach children and want to be successful at this. Most teachers are more than willing to give your child extra time, if they have it, to help the student.

But I must warn you that a teacher is only going to meet your child half way. They will not go to study hall and ask the student to come down to their class for help. They won't call your home to see if the child has questions. If teachers feel their time and energy is being wasted, they'll back off.

If it seems like I'm giving you a lot of information

encouraging you to seek outside assistance, it's not because you shouldn't tutor your child. However, I have some real concerns about parents tutoring because I've seen many problems with parents functioning like tutors over the years. It can place a tremendous strain on the parent-child relationship. I've seen children (and parents) almost to the point of tears with frustration. The parent wants the child to do well and conveys that message to the child. The child wants to please the parent. When things aren't going well, the parent gets frustrated and the child gets tense. There are many emotional factors that get thrown into the mix that only serve to complicate things.

When I was first employed as a psychologist a family came to me due to problems they were experiencing during "homework time." The student was in a program for learning disabled students and received small group instruction at school. The mother also spent time each evening working on math facts. At the time I was working with the family the student was trying to master his multiplication tables. Each evening things appeared to start out rather peacefully but typically degenerated into tears, yelling, foot stomping and pencil breaking. The student would become very angry with his mother due to what he perceived as unfair criticism. The mother was easily frustrated and had a tendency to take out this frustration on the boy. Within a short time they were at each others throats. Clearly this was not doing anything to improve the parent-child relationship and was not helping the child learn his multiplication tables either.

Another important point to consider is that parents aren't professional educators. By and large, parents lack expertise in crucial educational concepts and practical teaching skills. They haven't had training in teaching reading or math, and they have not had years of on the job experience. I've had more than a few parents tell me that they would be happy to tutor their son or daughter in Algebra if only they knew how to work the problems themselves! I can relate.

Another option for parents who do want to function as "the

tutor" is have the professionals at your school help you with a plan. They can give you specific techniques on how to teach your child spelling, how much time to work on math, and give some real guidance in these area. It is also a good idea to consult with your child's teachers before you begin a program so you aren't teaching the student a different process than being taught at school. The teacher has a certain way of solving a problem and the parent has another. In no time at all, the student is using parts of both systems and is totally confused. Meeting with the teacher can help prevent this type of situation from occurring.

Another problem which was alluded to earlier arises when parents become overly involved. Instead of it being the child's test, it becomes "our test." When parents assume too much of the responsibility, the student will sit back and let it happen. Parents are only trying to help but they end up hurting. Granted, it's done out of love but the child needs to hear loud and clear that **school is their responsibility**, not mom and dad's. I realize it is easy to get your own ego tied up with your child's accomplishments but try to avoid this. I understand that there is such a tremendous emotional bond between parent and child that these issues can become confusing. I recall a parent telling me, "Sometimes I think it's more important to me that my daughter does well than it is to her." If you took the "sometimes" out of the above sentence, it would be 100% accurate. It **was** more important to the parent than to the child and that was a big part of the problem.

Having put up, what I believe to be a pretty solid case **against** parents becoming involved as direct tutors, what are the arguments **for** parents tutoring their own children? It shows your child in no uncertain terms that education is important. It can't be stressed too strongly that it's not enough to tell your children that education is important, it had better be demonstrated. Actions speak louder than words!

I remember a fifth-grade student who seemed to struggle every year. You could look back through this child's cumulative folder and from kindergarten on the child had usually started the year in fine fashion and slowly declined until near the last quarter when he was doing very little. You could read the teacher's comments in the file and tell that this was a pattern. Nearly every spring there were special parent/teacher conferences to get at the problem.

I called the student into my office, and just as I had suspected, he suffered from Low Frustration Tolerance. As the weather got nicer, his work got sloppier. Eventually, he would be coming to school but was basically only occupying a chair. The school had tried keeping him in from recess, setting up special privileges if he completed his work, and other behavioral methods to change his habits, but nothing seemed to work.

I asked him what his parents thought about his difficulties and he said something to the effect that they didn't like it and thought he could do better. When I asked what happened to him when his report card came home with failing grades he said, "Not much. They grounded me for the semester. That usually lasts about a week. They take away my Nintendo for a few days but not much else." The child had learned that there were going to be no real consequences so why do all this boring homework? He knew he could wait out the punishment.

The story gets more interesting when, in seventh grade, the parents went through an ugly, drawn out divorce. For the good of the child it was decided he should live with his sister who actually lived in the same town. Truth be told I think both parents just wanted to have a break from the child who, as you may have guessed, was an excellent con man/manipulator. The sister was absolutely convinced that her brother needed to be "awakened" regarding the importance of school. She actually worked in my office where we talked numerous times about how she might be able to motivate him. I warned her that this was not going to be easy because this thirteen-year-old believed he could control adults. Let's face it, he had for thirteen years.

To make a long story shorter, there was a war in that home. Contracts were signed, notes were sent home, students were grounded, adults were in tears, and screaming and yelling were heard. The older sister, Cindy, held her ground and would not give in.

I asked her one day, "How are things going?" She told me he was starting to be more responsible. Books came home, the assignments got turned in, and he even asked for help with his homework. I wish I could end this story by telling you the child went on to Harvard or something, but I can't. He remained with his sister and did manage to finish high school from what I've learned. At the rate he was going there was not one chance in a hundred this student would have earned a high school diploma without the behavior management plan his sister implemented. I give credit to them both.

Let me assure you that this was an extreme case. Had it not been for the seven or eight years of not holding the student responsible for his behavior, the battle wouldn't have been so long and drawn out. That is why it's so important to set up healthy attitudes early.

Another positive result of tutoring your child is that it allows you to spend time together. Done in a healthy and cooperative manner, tutoring can help parents and children grow closer together. Having a common goal and working toward that goal can be a great experience. I've had parents tell me that the hour they set aside for school work can turn into a sort of "family time" where they talk over the days events after the work is done. It then becomes a nice way of illustrating that after the work is done, we enjoy a fun activity...first we work, then we play. This helps develop self-discipline and the ability to delay gratification which are the keys to success in nearly every endeavor.

Tutoring your child can be fun. You can learn a great deal. Some of the topics studied are extremely interesting. If you haven't been exposed to their curriculum, I think you might find some surprising changes. Tutoring programs such as these can indeed have many hidden benefits.

SIX
Reading:
From Phonics to Comics

Without a doubt, the most commonly occurring academic concerns are difficulties related to reading. Reading is so highly focused upon in the early grades that even if a child is performing adequately in all other subject areas, poor performance in reading is grounds for concern.

In early grades, much of the information is either given orally by the teacher or is read aloud by the entire class. If students are not good readers they can simply follow along as others read and still pick up the meaning. By middle school and high school, students are more or less on their own to gather the relevant information from a science or social studies chapter. If they are poor readers they are at a serious disadvantage in almost every class. Even when students have excellent calculation skills they may still struggle in math due to an inability to read story problems correctly.

Reading is gathering information through the printed word. The key phrase here is gathering information which implies comprehension or the ability to understand what is read. There are basically two primary skills involved in reading: 1)The ability to call or recognize words and 2) the ability to comprehend or understand what you have read. It is nearly impossible to be proficient at comprehending without being able to smoothly recognize the printed words. Occasionally you will see students who have such excellent skills at using context that even though they make numerous errors in reading, they can still figure out the main elements of a story. They still miss important details because of their dysfluency. Somehow they can logically think through what they've read and still gather a general understanding.

It is *not* uncommon to find students who read fluently but do not comprehend what they have read. They can read a paragraph and not miss a syllable yet when you ask what they have just read they haven't actually processed any of the information. Their eyes have gone over the material but they do not understand it.

Sound/symbol relationships are difficult for many as well. As a school psychologist whose primary responsibility is the diagnosis of learning and emotional problems, I have worked with literally hundreds of children who struggle with reading. A majority of these children have one common difficulty...they don't hear sound/symbol relationships. In other words, they can't "sound things out." For some reason they have a difficult time learning the association between a letter or a group of letters and the sounds they represent. Some can associate a letter with its sound when working with isolated letters. They run into difficulty when they are asked to blend letter sounds together. They can remember that an "s" has a sound like the beginning sound when you say "sing." But asks them to blend the beginning combinations in a word such as "string" and they are unable to do so. In educational terminology, sound/symbol relationships fall under an umbrella known as phonetic analysis or simply phonics.

Research suggests that approximately 10% of children (mostly boys) have difficulties learning to read phonetically. There is an ongoing debate over the importance of phonics. In one camp there are educators who believe phonics are the key to successful reading and any child who doesn't have a good grasp of phonics is likely to always be a poor reader. In the other camp there are educators who believe phonics are overemphasized. They argue that it is a confusing system with all the long and short vowel sounds. The English language has literally hundreds of words that do not follow the phonetical system and yet we learn to read these words with their silent letters and all.

The truth probably lies somewhere in the middle of these two positions regarding the importance of phonics. Most students who have poor phonetical skills are poor readers. However, students should not over rely on phonics to the point of sounding out every letter of every word. Students who use this approach ("letter by letter" readers) are also poor readers as they concentrate so hard on pronouncing the word they have difficulties comprehending what they have read.

Another important point to consider is that at a certain point we no longer rely on phonics to read. How many words have you sounded out while reading this book? As mature readers, you simply don't read the way you did when you were in 1st grade. Your eyes skim across the pages and you recognize each word or cluster of words as you go. That's how mature readers read, and it is clearly a very different process than sounding out letter sounds to make words. That is why I believe attention should be paid to phonics but only to give the student the requisite skills in this area before moving on.

There are many reasons students struggle with sound/ symbol relationships. One of the most common reason has to do with chronic ear infections at an earlier age. That is not to say that a single ear infection can cause this problem. I am referring to ongoing, long term cases where the child's ears seem to be continually filled with fluid.

Between the ages of approximately 18 to 48 months there are tremendous changes taking place in the child's brain. At this stage language is developing at a rapid pace. Experts in language acquisition refer to this period as a "critical stage" in development which means that during this time the area of the brain that is specialized in processing language (i.e. left temporal lobe) is developing and becoming highly specialized. In order for this area to develop to greatest efficiency requires a certain type of input or stimulation which in this case is language. If during this period they are denied input by having chronic ear infections the child's temporal lobe will fail to develop fully. The unfortunate fact about this process is that once that critical stage is passed, it is gone. No amount of stimulation at a later date can make up for the lack of language during that crucial time. The number of axons and dendritic connections found in the language processing center of the brain will have been permanently affected. I often see children who have suffered chronic ear infections who also have weak vocabulary skills and poor verbal reasoning skills. This includes a high percentage of students who later are diagnosed as learning disabled.

Research on determining which factor is the most accurate predictor of learning disabilities suggests that the severity and number of ear infections is one of the best predictors. This is after considering several factors known to be related to academic achievement such as intelligence, parent's educational background, parent's income, and the number of siblings in a family.

There are other causes of reading difficulties. The second most common cause is related to visual, perceptual problems. The words appear to "jump around on the page" or "flip flop" these children say. Many of these students are referred to as dyslexic. While the term "dyslexia" has become a buzz word used by the general public and media it is not used nearly as often by professionals because the meanings have become arbitrary. If we ask one hundred educators for their definition of dyslexia I'm confident very few would be the same.

Presently, using the term dyslexia usually leads to more confusion than understanding.

Students who have visual-perceptual deficits can often hear sounds adequately but have difficulty recognizing the letters or words. They reverse letters, see letters upside down or even flip flop entire words. Such difficulties are very common in 1st and 2nd grade. Reversing "b" and "d" at age seven is not cause for alarm. Even an occasional reversal in third grade is not unusual. Many students make occasional reversals with letters that are similar in appearance. Some just take a little longer to master this skill.

As I often tell parents, children are a lot like flowers...they bloom at different times. If your child is struggling with this skill it probably just means the child is taking a little longer than expected to bloom in this area. You can't speed this process by any means that I'm aware of because nature has its own timetable. When it's time, it will happen.

For students with the problems I just described I recommend the **Paired Reading Technique**. The best part about PRT is that it is simple, straightforward and seems to work regardless of who the helper happens to be. That is, the student appears to make approximately the same gains in reading whether the assistance is provided by a parent, teacher, or reading specialist. The support is in the process used by PRT and not in the age, gender, or IQ of the helper.

Paired Reading is a multi-sensory approach. It relies on more than one sense to encode the printed material. With a phonics only approach (i.e. sounding out), the student relies on auditory or hearing skills. In a sight word approach, the emphasis is almost totally on visual skills. With paired reading, both of these skills are used simultaneously as well as kinesthetic (muscle movement) skills. With this combination of senses students will hopefully rely on their stronger skills while not ignoring the skills that need improvement. Also, the more senses that are involved in the encoding process, the more senses the student has to rely upon during the recall phase of reading.

There is a tendency to approach academic skills deficits by spending too much time on overcoming a student's weaknesses. If a student has poor phonics skills, some believe there should be intense practice on these skills to gain adequate ability in phonetic analysis. Logically, this may make sense, but in practice this is not always a good strategy.

If the student has a deficit in phonetic analysis, there is a reason for that deficit. As pointed out, there are numerous reasons why a student may be unable to learn a certain skill such as phonics. There may have been very poor instruction. The student could have had significant health problems and missed school during this time frame. It is always possible that the student simply has had fluid in their ears. If, however, there has been considerable effort to help the student and they still "just don't get it," there is probably a neurological basis for the deficit. A deficit that is neurologically based will probably not respond to continued drill and practice. **It is much better to work around the weakness rather than to focus on it.** I wish we had the technology and know how to give students a pill or shot and make everything work the way it is suppose to but that just isn't possible. It is possible to teach the students to use their stronger skills in place of their weaker skills. If they have a weakness in phonics, they can learn to rely on their visual senses and vice versa.

As stated earlier, Paired Reading uses all three (visual, auditory and kinesthetic) learning channels simultaneously. The helper starts by sitting behind the child with their mouth fairly close to the student's right ear. The helper is going to be reading along with the student and the voice needs to be directed at the student's dominant ear. For approximately 90-95% of people, that is the right ear. The reading material should be at a level of difficulty so the student can read the material with some success but not a story they have memorized. Ideally, the material is at a level where they know 80-90% of the words.

The helper should start by trying to read aloud right along with the child. The helper's job is to set the pace and read each word exactly when the student reads the word. **When a student doesn't know a word there is no stopping to sound out the word.** Reading is done without hesitation. The idea is for the helper to set a moderate pace but not to stop and start every time the student doesn't know a word. Hopefully, the student will learn the words by hearing them read by the assistant or helper.

Another important part of Paired Reading is for the child to run his or her hand under the line of words being read. It is often a good idea for the helper to place a hand over the child's hand to control the pace. After the system is learned it is usually possible to let the child move a hand under the words independently.

If the student appears to be able to handle the material with a minimum of mistakes the helper can stop reading aloud and simply follow along. If they start to have difficulties it is time to start reading aloud again.

A slight variation on this theme is what is called "Popcorn Reading." The helper and student read a book together but only one person is reading aloud. The individual reading aloud says "popcorn," which is the cue for the other person to start reading aloud. This technique is a way to make certain the student is following along when they aren't reading aloud.

At the end of a paragraph it is a good idea to see if the child has understood what was read. Comprehension is usually improved with this approach because dysfluent readers are reading with improved accuracy. As stated earlier, "choppy" readers often lose the meaning of what they have read.

In many ways learning to read is like learning to speak. Students learn by approximations of accuracy, not immediate perfection. It is better to have a child reread a sentence or paragraph to determine if they can comprehend the meaning the second time. Then they can be verbally praised for discovering the meaning. More success is built into reading that way. It is also a good idea to make mental notes as you go of which words the student missed the first time through a passage.

Then go back and re-read a passage later to determine if

the same mistakes are made again or if the unfamiliar words are being learned. Continually missed words can be put on flash cards.

One advantage of Paired Reading is that it seems to flow fairly smoothly. There is no time for the student to feel frustrated as they try to sound out words. It is just reading a story together and nearly anyone can learn to be a helper. Moms, Dads, teachers, grandparents and even big brothers and sisters can be capable assistants.

Another technique to use with a student is actually a procedure to teach them to rely on context to learn unfamiliar words. They can learn to use on their own if an assistant is unable to provide direct support.

In this approach when a student is faced with an unfamiliar word, he or she makes the beginning letter sound for that word and reads to the end of the sentence. By the end of the sentence there hopefully have been enough cues or hints to help the student figure out the unfamiliar word.

Let's say a sentence read, "Bobby was on the water in a boat." If the student is unable to read the word "water" he or she is to make the "w" sound and read to the end of the sentence. By the end of the sentence the student is to try and figure out what the "w" word could be. If the student can conceptualize that the person in the sentence is "on" something and in a "boat," a logical guess would be "water" for the unfamiliar word. "Water" has a "w" and you can also hear the "er" at the end. "Water," then, must be the word missed.

The idea here is that if a student stops at each unfamiliar word the valuable contextual information that comes after the unfamiliar word is missed. Many times the unfamiliar word is obvious by reading to the end of the sentence.

An important part of helping dysfluent readers become better readers has to do with giving appropriate and timely cues. Students should be allowed to discover their own mistakes. Many times when they substitute an incorrect word they will recognize that what they have read doesn't make sense. If they do correct themselves, they need praise ("You did a good job of finding your mistake.") At the end of a paragraph it is good to help them discover how they figured out what was wrong. ("How did you know that word was 'father' instead of 'dad'?") It is important to reinforce the student's attempts at self-corrections whether they are successful or not. Self-corrections lead to increased independence which should be nurtured. As stated earlier, a relationship with a parent assuming responsibility for the student's difficulties is not desired. You can praise their attempts at self-corrections even if the attempts are incorrect by stating things like, "I noticed you tried _____ when you had trouble. Good job."

Other cues to help with unfamiliar words are drawing attention to a picture ("Does what you read match the picture?") Many times the sentence structure can provide clues to the word ("You said _____. Does that make sense?") Obviously, the visual cues of the letters are valuable ("Does that look right?") If a child has a habit of missing the beginnings or endings of words, it is good to draw attention to these areas with cues like "Do you know a word that begins/ends with those letters?" You can encourage the child to seek clues to the unfamiliar word by drawing attention to the letter/sound cues. ("What sounds can you see in that word? Now, what's a word that would make sense which has those sounds?") Much of the information in Chapter 6 is taken from a book by Marie Clay (1986) entitled *Early Detection of Reading Difficulties*. For more detailed information please refer to this excellent resource.

A point that I want to make is that **children of any age love being read to.** For some reason once children are too big to sit on a lap adults no longer read to them. Helpers can read to students or have students read to them at any age. This is a fun activity for children and can provide some much needed quiet time for parents and students.

Reading Comprehension

There are several techniques that can be very helpful for students who have difficulties comprehending what they have read. Usually students struggle with comprehension because they are failing to concentrate on what they are reading. We've all had the experience of reading a page then having no idea of the information just read.

Two solid techniques for improving comprehension are using predictions and relating the story to the child. At the end of a page simply ask the child, "What do you think will happen next?" This prediction causes the child to process what has happened previously and draw inferences as to what might happen later. I also like to ask if their prediction came true when they have continued with the story.

Another good technique is for the helper to ask the child a question at the end of the page and then have the child ask the helper a question. In order to ask a question the student has to understand what has occurred on the proceeding page.

To determine whether or not the student has comprehended what they have read have them paraphrase the material. Paraphrasing also helps the student process the passage at a deeper level and helps in retrieval of the material. By putting the material they have read in their own words children are forced to process the story a second time.

Another "trick" to aid in comprehension is relating the story to the child. Ask the child "What would you have done?" "Does this remind you of the time you…?" One of the oldest tricks in an accounting class is to tell the students who are careless with their balance sheets to "pretend this is your money." By relating the story to the child it immediately becomes more interesting and the child will pay closer attention. Let's face it…we are all more interested in ourselves than just about anyone else we know. That's especially true of children.

Reading Difficulties in Middle and High School

If you are the parent of a middle or high school aged student, the previous information may still be relevant to you. Some teenagers are still reading at third and fourth grade levels. Chances are, if that is the case, your child is receiving individual instruction as part of a learning disabilities or remedial reading program.

If your child is not receiving specialized instruction but is still struggling there is a very basic recommendation I'd like to offer. **Somehow you need to get your child to spend time reading.** I know that is easier said than done. Most people don't like doing things they are not good at because it's frustrating. As I stated in the introduction, I detest trying to fix things and want to spend a minimum amount of time on such activities. I also realize that if I am ever to improve in this area I will have to learn to tolerate this frustration.

As I review this chapter I realize I have not discussed a major motivation for reading....pleasure. Somehow we have to help children learn that reading can be fun. One of the ways this can be facilitated is by allowing the reader to have as much control as possible. Allow students to select what books they would like to read. Encourage them to read books that are somewhat hard for them. A trap many readers fall into is only wanting to read books that are easy. The problem is most great literature does not fall into the "easy" category. Students select books they are comfortable reading but find these books boring and then overgeneralize the belief that reading is boring.

One idea to encourage reading is to pick a time during the evening when everyone reads. It can be a short as 15 minutes but the only thing going on during that time is reading. As stated earlier, the student has the freedom to choose any material as long as they are reading. There are programs like this in schools where, for example, from 2:00 to 2:20 P.M. **everyone** in the school reads. In our school this is called D.E.A.R time which stands for "Drop Everything and Read."

Virtually any reading is beneficial. Students do not have to be reading Shakespeare to be improving their reading skills. For that reason I encourage parents to provide their children with whatever reading material their children will read. By this I mean subscriptions to auto body magazines, *Sports Illustrated*, *Teen*, comic books, or anything else they like. Allowing freedom is important but having a variety of material to choose from is also vital in fostering a love of reading. Research has shown that 90% of the students in top reading groups are or were heavy comic book readers who graduated to more complicated material. So go up to the attic or down to the basement and dig out your old Green Lantern or Superman comics!

As mentioned earlier, most of the school districts in this country have reading specialists. Parents should contact the school and set up a meeting to discuss their son or daughter's reading difficulties with these professionals. Chances are they have some excellent ideas and resources at their disposal.

A majority today have home computers or at least have access to a computer. There is some excellent software to teach reading comprehension. Many of the students who hate to read love computers so this might be an avenue to explore. Local school districts or public libraries may be a starting place. Many of these programs can be borrowed or checked out of the school or library. Why not let them have fun on a computer while they are improving their reading skills?

SEVEN
Spelling:
A Multisensory Approach

Spelling can be a difficult subject for many and can take up a lot of study time during the week. Many argue that too much emphasis is placed on spelling. They stress that with the technology available today (i.e. computer spelling assistance), more emphasis should be placed on thinking skills and less on tasks that are basically a function of rote memorization like spelling. Agree or disagree, the reality of the situation is that spelling will be a part of elementary curricula for the foreseeable future. The task now is to find a systematic means of remediating poor spelling skills and dealing with the frustration that spelling can bring.

If your child has a difficult time with spelling, the following plan may help. The best thing about this plan is that it's consistent, easy to follow, and requires spaced practice over the week. It is also done, for the most part, alone by the student which will hopefully foster independence in the child.

Before I explain a systematic approach to overcoming deficits in spelling, let me share with you a simple procedure for determining a student's dominant learning style. Everyone has a dominant modality, a means of processing information that comes easier to us. Some rely on visual skills and "see" things in their mind's eye. They prefer to look at graphs and charts to take in information. Most of these individuals are what some people refer to as "right hemisphere dominant." The phrase is actually somewhat of a misnomer since such an expression gives the impression that one hemisphere in the brain is working while the other hemisphere is not. In actuality the two hemispheres work in conjunction virtually all of the time unless an individual has had the bundle of nerves connecting the two hemispheres surgically severed. The right hemisphere tends to be specialized for artistic processes, visual/spatial problem solving, creativity, as well as the expression and reception of emotions.

There are other individuals who rely on auditory skills. They would much rather listen while information is explained to them. The dominant hemisphere with a majority of auditory learners is the left hemisphere. This hemisphere appears to be specialized for language, analytical thought, and processing symbolic material.

Still others rely on tactile/kinesthetic skills. They are most comfortable when they can physically handle and manipulate objects. All individuals use combinations of these modalities at certain times. The point is that everyone has a modality they feel most comfortable with and would prefer to use. When instruction is tailored to that dominant learning style, the results can be dramatic.

My wife and I are an interesting contrast. I am very much an auditory learner. I can see a movie once and recite the dialogue from an entire scene. I learn things most efficiently when they are explained to me verbally. For me to make use of a chart or graph I first have to figure out the chart and convert the information into words. Don't ever have me navigate or try to use a map. In fact, don't rely on me to find the car outside of a K-Mart! When coming off an elevator I am the type of person who invariably turns the wrong way.

My wife is a visual learner. She can look at a chart and gather all of the relevant information from it in a few seconds. She can almost always tell you which direction is north, south, east, or west. Is it any surprise she is a graphic artist?

There are a few simple tricks to determine if a student is a visual or auditory learner. Ask them to spell a word and watch their eyes. If their eyes move horizontally, they are probably auditory learners. By their eyes moving left or right along a horizontal plane they are activating the areas of the brain that process sound (i.e. the temporal lobes). If their eyes shift up toward the ceiling, they are probably visual learners. By their eyes shifting up they are, in effect, trying to "see" the word in their mind's eye.

Ask the student the following :

1) Would you (the student) remember a story better by listening to it on a cassette or seeing it on a video tape?

2) Could you tell a better story or write and draw a better story?

3) Do you learn the best by reading something to yourself or having someone read something to you?

Younger students probably can not answer these questions with any real definitiveness but by high school most students have a sense of how they prefer to learn. If they don't it may be something worth exploring through an evaluation which will be discussed in a following chapter.

It's not that a visual approach is better or worse than an auditory approach. In fact, individuals who are proficient at spelling typically use both auditory and visual retrieval techniques. The more channels a student can use to recall information, the better.

Have you ever written a word and somehow the word just didn't look right? This is a good example of a visual approach to spelling. It is also appropriate to have students recheck a word to make certain they have written all the letters they can hear in the word. That is not to say students should be taught to over rely on phonetic analysis for spelling. The English language is such an irregular language with numerous exceptions that many words simply have to be memorized.

When the weekly spelling words come home, before any studying begins, the student should be given a pre-test to determine what words they can already spell correctly. Besides determining words to concentrate on, it can also identify error patterns to be corrected After the pre-test has been completed, start with the first word on the list and follow these steps:

Step 1) Have the student copy the word one time.

Step 2) Have the student write the word three times while saying the sounds the letters are making. Try to get the child to stretch out the word so that they are saying the sounds as they are writing them.

Step 3) Have the student touch each letter while saying the letter name. They should say the entire word after the last letter is spoken.

Step 4) Have them turn the paper over and write the word. Then compare to see if the word is spelled correctly.

Step 5) Go on to the next word and complete steps 1-4.

After they have finished the second word have the student close his or her eyes and recall the first word. Have the student write the word and say each letter out loud as they write it.

The student can learn this routine and can soon study independently. After they have completed the steps they can be given a practice test. Once all the words are spelled correctly they only need to review the words for a few minutes each night.

Often times students are fairly consistent in their spelling mistakes. It might be a good idea to look for patterns in the student's errors and help them correct the problem. It is also true that in early elementary grades the spelling list usually has a "theme" for each week. One week the theme may be that a majority of words have "ar" or end with "ed." Make certain the student recognizes these themes. Knowing this information can help them when it comes time for the exam on Friday.

The key to an effective spelling program is spaced practice using a multi-sensory approach. From the above description, the student has the opportunity to practice for a short time over a few days and uses visual, auditory, and kinesthetic channels.

For students in early elementary grades there is a technique that can be helpful in getting students to separate words into segments by the sounds they hear. The technique involves drawing boxes for the student according to the number of sounds contained in a word. For example, the word "make" has three sounds; the "m" sound, the "a" sound, and the "k" or "c" sound. Make three boxes for the student and then draw a dotted line down the third box and place the silent "e" in this newly created fourth box. Have the student try to figure out what sound they hear first and put the letter that makes that sound in the first box. Then proceed by asking the student what sound they hear next for the second box, etc. It is also appropriate to fill in other silent letters or to give them assistance with skills they haven't learned yet.

A suggestion to both teachers and parents as a way to improve the likelihood of the spelling list making it home is to give the student extra credit if they bring the list back with a parent's signature. For example, you can give the student ten extra credit points for bringing back a signed list. In that way the student can miss a word but still receive 100% on the exam. The real bonus to this simple plan is that it gives the student a reason to get the words home to his or her parents so that practice can begin.

A common concern with poor spellers is that they can learn the words for the spelling test but will then misspell the same words the following week. The learning hasn't generalized from the testing environment to everyday usage of the words. On each new spelling list include three words that were misspelled from last week's list. This has to be done individually for each student since the students will not have missed the same words. If the student received 100% last week then they can choose any three words from last week's list. This helps a student become a better speller by focusing on words they are still struggling with and, in effect, gives them an extra week to practice these words.

With older students, it is probably not a wise use of energy to spend a lot of time working on spelling skills. As mentioned earlier, with the technology available today there are "spell checkers" built into nearly every computer. While some people view spell checkers as a crutch or as cheating, they actually can improve spelling. Some computers have a spelling option of having the computer make a special sound if a word is misspelled. The student gets immediate feedback on which words are misspelled and hopefully will learn to spell the word correctly the next time they use it.

Another handy tool is something called a spelling dictionary. These dictionaries do not have any definitions of words, just the words themselves. They are small and can be carried in a back pack or even a Trapper Keeper. A student can look up the correct spelling in a few seconds.

Playing games such as Scrabble or Boggle can help spelling skills dramatically. These games are a nice change of pace from the standard drill and practice that spelling requires. Spelling is no longer a subject, per se, at the high school level but students are still expected to be able to spell. Using games is a way to focus on improving spelling after the days of weekly spelling lists are long gone.

EIGHT
Mathematics:
Manipulatives, Fractions,
and Phobias

Helping a student who is struggling with math is probably more straightforward than helping one who is struggling with other subject areas. To learn to be a good math student, you have to spend time learning the correct procedures which means there needs to be practice working problems. That holds true today in much the same way it was true when Pythagoras and Euclid were practicing mathematics a few of thousand years ago. There are no short cuts that make this process any easier today. Even with the use of calculators, the student still has to understand the logic of the problem solving technique.

The study of mathematics is different from the study of other disciplines in one significant sense. Mathematics is a process by which new skills are continually being added to previously learned skills. It seems as if each week involves a new concept or at least a new procedure to be learned to solve a new type of problem. Given the nature of mathematics, there is a great deal of time where the student is somewhat confused or "lost" as they seek total understanding. Each new concept or skill requires the student spend time seeking understanding. In a class such as science, social studies, or history, there is much less time spent dealing with this process and therefore much less anxiety to tolerate. I don't think I've ever heard the phrase "history anxiety" because learning history is a very different process. Information is presented and the student is asked to understand the information, draw inferences about the significance of the events, explain how the events might have been different today, or demonstrate their understanding through other means. Their ability to perform these tasks falls somewhere on a continuum but rarely is it the case that the student is totally unable to perform any of these tasks. They may know very little about the War of 1812 but it is hard to believe a student can be in a half dozen lectures and not know a thing about the war. The anxiety with a class like history is usually over the "big exam" or "big paper."

With mathematics, however, things tend to be much more black or white. A student either has the knowledge to complete the problem or does not. Completing five or six steps of a problem is insufficient if the problem requires eight steps to be completed correctly. It feels like a disaster not to get the answer. If students can name five of the six factors that lead to the War of 1812 they could answer the question and feel like a success. This answer might even be considered a good answer. With math it is more a case of all or nothing. Good math students have to learn to tolerate the frustration and anxiety the subject can bring.

Elementary School

For students in early elementary school who are struggling in math I highly recommend using manipulatives which are objects the student can physically handle. This can be anything from jelly beans to pennies to cutting up an apple to teach about fractions.

Manipulatives are a great way of getting across the basic concepts involved in mathematics. In its purest sense, mathematics starts with an amount or number. Some process (addition, subtraction, multiplication, or division) is performed and the amount changes. For example, there are five apples. If one gets taken away, there are only four apples. That is the very essence of mathematics, and it can not be demonstrated in any clearer fashion than by using manipulatives and actually performing the problem before the student's eyes.

Using coins to teach mathematics is an excellent technique because it has real world relevance that will help students focus their attention. You can teach all the basic mathematical operations with pennies, nickels, dimes, and quarters.

When teaching a student about fractions, don't hesitate to cut up an apple or better yet, use a real pie. If they answer correctly they can sample a real reward. With a pie cut into eight pieces ask the student, "How many pieces will we have to eat to have ¾ of the pie left?" Having a motivated (and hungry) learner never hurt the educational process.

Another age old technique that still stands the test of time is the use of flash cards. Flash cards can be used with simple addition and subtraction facts all the way up through multiplication and division tables. When a procedure has been used for years and years there is usually a very good reason for using it. Usually it's because the procedure works well!

There is a flash card game that students seem to enjoy too, where you start with all the cards on a chain. The cards should be in a random order and it is a good idea every other day or so to take the cards off the chain and shuffle them. The game is played by simply going through the cards each day. If the student answers correctly there is a "+" mark placed on the back of the card. If they answer incorrectly a "-" is placed on the back. Once a student gets three "plus" marks in a row the card is taken off the chain and put on the student's chain. Placing the card on their chain demonstrates that the card is mastered and they now own it. It's a nice way of visually showing the progress the student is making. Eventually all of the cards belong to the student and should be reviewed once every other week or so to make certain the skills aren't lost.

To add a little variety to flash cards it is possible to play "Beat the Clock." Have the student try to answer the questions as quickly as possible and keep track of the time required with a stop watch. The goal is to encourage automatic responses. If a student is going on to middle school and still has to stop and think about basic facts then it is fair to say that they could use additional practice with such skills.

There are several games that can be modified to become math games. You can take a checkers board and on each square write a math problem. Before a player can move to that square they must know the answer to the square's problem. If they can not answer the problem they have to move to a square where they do know the correct answer.

If the student has been working on basic math facts and can't seem to memorize them it could be that the student is suffering from a long term memory deficit. Later there will be a discussion of memory aids. It is also possible and more likely that the student is suffering from another difficulty that was touched upon earlier…math anxiety.

Everyone is aware of math anxiety to a certain extent because most people experience it at some time. With some it happens in second grade and with others it happens when a professor is trying to explain linear regression. That little voice in the back of the head says, "I'm not getting this!" Panic sets in and without realizing it the emphasis has been shifted away from the problem on the board and is now focused on the confusion, frustration, and anxiety the learner feels. During this time there can be no learning because all attention needed for understanding is focused on the feelings of anxiety. Often times these feelings of anxiety turn into feelings of anger so even more confusion and frustration follows.

You may recall from our discussion of rational-emotive behavior therapy (REBT) that there are two types of beliefs: 1) rational and 2) irrational. These beliefs are typically contained in our self-talk or internal dialogue. When discussing math anxiety it is not uncommon for both rational and irrational beliefs to go on simultaneously. The first part of the student's inner voice states "I'm not getting this" which is probably true and quite rational. When students believe they are confused, they are almost always correct. When they are asked to demonstrate a problem and have no idea the steps to take, they obviously weren't getting it. However, the fact that the student is not comprehending the process is not the source of the anxiety. There is a second part of this self-talk that usually is not apparent but is lurking just below the level of awareness. This second part usually goes something like this: "I'm not getting this and that's the worst thing in the world."

It is this second part that is irrational and produces anxiety. It is irrational because 1) Not understanding a math problem is far from the worst thing in the world. 2) To feel anxious over a math problem really isn't a legitimate threat to the student's well being. 3) If a student changed the second thought to "I'm not getting this but I probably will later. Even if I don't, it won't kill or maim me," it would create less anxiety.

So what do you do if the student you are working with exhibits signs of the math anxiety? There are several things that can be done to help.

1) Make the student(s) realize that eventually they'll look back on these problems and laugh at how uptight they were because now they can do them with ease.

2) Talk to a counselor who specializes in anxiety disorders. Typically, in a few sessions, the student can learn to cope effectively with their anxiety producing thoughts.

3) It is also possible to help them learn stress reduction techniques at home.

I used these techniques as part of a practicum experience at the University of Northern Iowa where they had a Learning Center that provided free tutoring. The tutors were graduate students who gained experience working closely with children who had learning and/or emotional problems. Parents used the clinic as a resource for tutorial assistance and the graduate students benefited by not having to track down their own clients.

My very first client was Chad, a fifth grade student with significant problems in math. After nearly two years of work, this student still did not know his multiplication tables. He had received literally hundreds of individual drill and practice sessions with his parents and school staff.

When Chad first entered the clinic, he was given a battery of tests and was found to be functioning with average intelligence. It didn't take me long to realize that if numerous other individuals had tried the flash card drill and practice techniques and it hadn't worked for them, it probably wouldn't work for me. I didn't know what to do, but I realized that a new approach was probably in order since the standard approaches hadn't worked.

You could literally see a change come over Chad once we started working on math. He became like a bar of steel, he was so uptight. Anyone could see that he had an extreme case of math anxiety. After ten minutes he literally had beads of sweat on his upper lip.

My professor, Dr. Schmitz, explained that Chad's level of anxiety was well above his ability in mathematics. It didn't really matter what his math skills were because his attention was being focused on his anxiety. Until his anxiety level was reduced to a point where it was at least even with his mathematics ability, this child was probably never going to master his multiplication tables. My professor suggested deep muscle relaxation training and taught me this simple technique in a few minutes.

Deep muscle relaxation starts by having the student tighten and relax various muscle groups. The trainer leads the process by having the student focus his or her attention on specific muscle groups until slowly and systematically reaching a very deep state of relaxation. It is important to realize that a state of deep relaxation is incompatible with the feeling of anxiety. It is impossible to be deeply relaxed and anxious at the same time.

The student starts with the toes and proceeds up the body.

The student tightens foot muscles for approximately ten seconds and then relaxes. All during this process the student is becoming more and more relaxed. Next the calf muscles, thighs, and stomach are tightened and relaxed until they've done every muscle group including the face and forehead. By this point the student should be noticeably less tense. Breathing should be slowed down and deep. Any physical signs of anxiety such as a tightened jaw should be absent. Once the student is totally relaxed, it is time to work on the multiplication facts. The student is encouraged to stay relaxed during the question and answer segment. It is best for students to keep their eyes closed while answering the questions.

Chad and I spent several weeks with little or no progress, and I was getting pretty discouraged. I was beginning to think this was a waste of time. Then one day something amazing happened. Chad got 23 of 25 problems correct instead of his usual 8 or 9. The next day he did just as well. His performance remained high and he started to gain a sense of confidence. You could almost hear his self-talk regarding math change from "I can't do this" to "I can do this." Once students believe they will have success, they will. Expecting to do well is more than half the battle.

Once Chad's anxiety level was lowered enough that it was no longer interfering with his skills, he did fantastically well. In a fourteen week period Chad made two years' progress in math. He didn't have a math disability, he had a severe case of math anxiety that was holding him back. Once he gained a sense of confidence regarding his math skills he actually seemed to enjoy math. At least he no longer feared it. Chad went on to use the muscle relaxation techniques we had worked on before tests at school, and at last contact was doing quite well.

High School

During later grades, the process of helping with math can be complicated by several factors. One of the factors that must be considered is can the tutor do the problems? We all remember our parents saying, "Wow…it's been twenty years since I've done this." At some point the parents may have been able to deal with quadratic equations but at this point, they are a mystery. As a parent it is perfectly acceptable to admit that you don't remember the steps in the process. The question is are you willing to take the time to relearn the process? If the answer is yes, then hit the books!

Even if algebra is too complicated there are still ways for parents to help their children. As has been explored in depth, hire a tutor. Reread the section on finding tutors…colleges, peers, and an ad in the newspaper is also a possibility.

Another source of assistance may be found at the local video store. In some of the larger chain stores (Blockbuster Video, etc.) there are videos on advanced math skills such as algebra and trigonometry. What an excellent way to provide a student with support. Since individuals in the home control the VCR, it is virtually impossible for the instructional pace to be either too fast or too slow. The tape can always be stopped and rewound if there are sections that are unclear.

If the parents decide to tutor math directly, my advice is very simple…work problems. The best way to solidify math skills is to practice, practice, practice. Math isn't learned by lecture or discussion. Math is learned by doing.

Don't be overly concerned with finding "the answer." It is more important to have a firm grasp of the process necessary to solve the problem correctly. Everyone likes to have the answer because that's the goal. However, if a student has the answer but doesn't understand the process, the stage has been set for future problems. Also, many times students working on math problems are able to repeat the process but do not know why the process works. When they run into a problem that requires a slight variation in the problem solving steps, they are unable to make the required adjustment because they don't really understand the logic of the procedure. The real reason for even working problems is to learn. It's really not about getting the "answer" but getting the "understanding." If the student keeps that in mind, they'll be in good shape.

NINE
General Techniques to Promote Achievement

An underachiever is a student who is not operating with maximum efficiency when it comes to school work. If an underachiever's performance was charted during the day as is often done by businesses to measure worker effectiveness, the lack of productivity would be shocking. Time is wasted, papers are lost, and valuable information is missed. In order to get back on track they need to learn new ways of handling their "job" (i.e. school).

Note taking is one of the most important skills a child can learn. Certainly by middle school and usually by upper elementary grades students will be expected to gather information through teacher lectures. Teaching note taking skills is so important that it warrants special consideration in this book. Taking good notes is not as difficult as it may seem. For an underachiever the biggest obstacles are motivation and organization. The good news is that taking good notes is a learnable skill that nearly everyone can master. No technique or device known to man will magically filter the information through the ear, to the hand, out the pencil, and onto the paper. Students need to learn this skill.

There is always the option of taping a lecture. I fully support the idea of using tape recorders. However, this may be a problem for several reasons: 1) It doesn't look "cool" to other students. A high percentage of underachievers are almost anti-achievement because they have the attitude that if they appear to really want to do well, it will ruin their image as a non-conformist. They wouldn't mind doing well but in case they do fail they don't want it to appear they put a significant effort into their work. 2) Once they tape the lecture, they will put the tape away and never listen to it again. 3) Because they are taping, they won't listen during the lecture. They will have a tendency to feel like they don't need to pay attention because now they have a tape of what was covered and they can learn this material anytime they choose. See # 2 above for the reason this often is not the case.

If a student does tape a lecture, I recommend having them take notes over the material at home where they can start and stop the tape. They should also take notes over the lecture soon after taping it while the information from class is still fresh in their memory. If they wait a week to take notes over a lecture they are apt to lose little bits and pieces of the material as the memory traces fade.

A good general suggestion is to tell the student to write the recorded information in their own words. I find this technique is an excellent means of encoding information at a deeper level and also aids in the recall of information. The process of transferring the information to their own words is helpful because 1) the student uses auditory skills by listening to the lecture. 2) The student then verbally processes the information in a unique way putting it in their own words. To be able to do this one has to really understand what is being presented.

It is possible to simply write down what the teacher says but this information has not been encoded. It simply has been copied down. 3) Finally, the student has to copy the lecture utilizing the tactile/kinesthetic channel. While writing notes students can't help but re-read what they have written which only reinforces the information they are trying to learn. If the teacher can get students to try programs like this, it is extremely surprising if their comprehension of the subject matter does not improve drastically.

Before beginning to help the students learn to be better note takers it's important students understand the importance of taking good notes. They are usually aware that knowing what the teacher talked about in class is important but they often don't realize that a majority of materials on a test is taken from the teacher's lectures. What the teacher feels is important is usually the focus in class and on exams.

Sometimes a simple contract system designed to give rewards for each page of notes taken works. This encourages students to take more detailed notes and also provides the opportunity to monitor their progress. For example, they can be given a point per page of notes and these points can be used to "buy" later curfew times, extra credit points or what ever else they would work toward. It's something to consider at least.

The first step in becoming a proficient note taker is learning to discern the main idea. Some students seem to have an inability to tell essential from non-essential detail. Let's consider a science class discussing how trees distribute water. The central point may be that the root system is the source of gathering and distributing water. To record the main idea it may only be necessary to write a short phrase or even a single word.

"Roots—gather and distribute water."

Once the central point is recorded listing illustrations is helpful. Students should be taught to use only as many words as is absolutely necessary to help recall a fact. It is not important to write down verbatim what was said. Focus on short phrases that will bring the information back later.

Roots—gather and distribute water.

branch out
up to 20 sq. ft.
anchor the tree

The above short phrases could convey all of the relevant information in that portion of the lecture. If there is time to write more and produce better examples it is advisable to do so. The important point is not to completely miss any of the information.

The use of abbreviations is also a great way to save time. I was in a neuropsychology class that contained a tremendous amount of information. Each weekly class period I wrote for two and one half hours and left with cramps in my hand. Everyone developed their own personal form of shorthand for the course. Neuropsychology = NP, Frontal Lobes = FL, etc. After a few weeks my note book looked like a secret code but it made perfect sense to me. Encourage students to use any tricks they want as long as they understand what the abbreviations mean. They need to experiment and learn for themselves what is helpful and what is not.

Another key to taking good notes is editing notes. Most write notes but never look them over until it is time to study. Students can look over their notes the day they take them and fill in missing parts, cross out portions that are confusing, make additional notes in the margins, or whatever will clarify the information. This only takes a few minutes, but can be very helpful later. If the student waits often times the notes don't make sense.

As already emphasized, studying for a short time each night is much more effective than cramming the night before the exam. If you can convince students to review their notes each night before bed (even if for only ten minutes) their retention will be higher.

While the material covered in class will undoubtedly be a priority on exams, there will also be information on exams that comes only from the reading. Most teachers aren't the least bit sneaky about what will be emphasized on the test. It is not uncommon for a teacher to say, "There will be a question on Bunker Hill. Know what happened there!" To answer the question completely the student will have to be able to draw information from the assigned readings.

There is a technique known as SQ3R designed to help students understand and recall material.

S = Survey
Q = Question
R = Read
R = Recall
R = Review

Survey

The student first looks through the chapter before reading. They should look at the pictures, important subheadings, and the summary if one is available. The idea is to get a basic idea of the content of the chapter. Setting the stage before reading helps create a "mental set" that helps the student process the information more efficiently. This process need not take more than a few minutes.

Question

Students look at each section of a chapter and prepare a few questions that will be answered as the chapter is read. Using our example of trees and roots, appropriate questions might be:

How do trees gather water?

What else do roots do?

Why are they necessary?

Many chapters have review questions at the end of the chapter. It is a good idea to go through these questions before beginning because they will point out the key points in the chapter.

Read

Now the student is ready to read the chapter. It should be read keeping the generated questions in mind. Earlier we defined reading as gathering information through printed material. If students aren't gathering information they aren't truly reading.

Recall

Once the student has finished the chapter it is time to determine how much is remembered by using the recorded questions. Without looking back through the book, the student should try to recall the answers to the questions. If the student can't recall the information it is important to re-read those sections.

Review

Next the students attempt to mentally review the material from each subheading without referring back to the their notes. When they have exhausted their recall, they can use the reading or their notes remembering that the notes won't be available come exam time. A common mistake is for students to think they know the material because they know their notes. However, they have never tried to recall the material without the use of their notes. Without the cues provided by the notes they actually don't know the material well enough to recall it spontaneously and they have a tough time with the exam.

Another technique to help students learn the information in a chapter is to simply take notes over the reading. This is effective for the reasons mentioned before: 1) requires the use of visual, auditory, and tactile/kinesthetic channels 2) rewording passages causes processing and conceptualization at a deeper level. This takes time but nothing works better for learning the information presented in a text.

The Use of Games

Another topic worth mentioning is the use of games to facilitate learning. There are board games available for nearly every conceivable academic skill: multiplication tables, fractions, reading comprehension, spelling, geography etc. I'd encourage parents to go to the school and ask about games available to be checked out. Teachers are usually glad to loan games and can also tell parents where to buy them.

Using games is an excellent technique to improve weaker skills because kids love playing games, and it makes studying fun. Whenever possible, it's best not to focus on the fact that they're learning. The focus should be on having fun and the learning process will take care of itself. Students will spend more time studying this way and, hopefully, will have a better attitude toward the subject matter. There are even games you can play in the car on long trips that are educational. As a young child I recall working on the alphabet by picking out letters from road signs. Whoever saw the letter first got to claim it as their own. The winner in this game was the first person to make it from A to Z.

There are two distinct game activities that can be used with a wide variety of subjects. The first is good old Tic-Tac-Toe. For this example I'll use the subject matter of spelling but this format can be used with virtually any subject: math, reading, science, or social studies all work quite well.

After drawing the game squares ask the student to spell one of the words from the spelling list for that week. If they spell the word correctly they get to put an "X" in one of the boxes. The next player can either write the word correctly or misspell it. The other player has to tell whether that word is correctly spelled or not. If it is incorrect, he or she has to spell it correctly to put another "X" in a box. If the student states the word is incorrect when it is correct or fails to spell the word correctly, the adult gets to put an "O" in a box. The output portion can be rotated by either spelling the word on paper, out loud, or both.

Another hidden benefit of the game is that it teaches thinking skills and strategy. If more than one child is playing they can have them compete against each other using their own spelling words.

The second game that works quite well is Jeopardy. It is easy to construct a Jeopardy game board with two large sheets of construction paper with horizontal slits cut in the front layer. The number of columns may depend on how many categories to be incorporated into the game. For this example, let's use the Jeopardy game to work on math skills. There could be a column or "category" for addition, subtraction, multiplication, division, and fractions. The questions become increasingly difficult as they increase in dollar value ($100 through $500 for each category). Questions are written on index cards and players take turns reading and answering questions. If students answer the question correctly, they get the card and receive credit for the question's dollar amount just as in Jeopardy. If students miss the question either the question can be removed from the board or placed back into the game so there is a chance to solve it again at a later time. This is a fun game to play. Students might even invite classmates over for Jeopardy tournaments. The class can be divided into two teams for a special activity. Hopefully, this demonstrates the versatility of games for a wide variety of subjects.

Spelling words can simply be placed on index cards for the week. As the year goes along there is a longer and longer list of words from which to draw. The weeks spelling words should be placed in the positions of higher value since they haven't been practiced previously.

With reading it is simply a matter of using flash cards for words the student is trying to learn. Games can be used to work on comprehension skills by writing short passages and then asking questions that require making inferences. For example, a passage might read, "Sandy wanted to leave for school, but was not able to find her shoes. She looked all over the house and still couldn't find them. Suddenly she remembered that she had gone into the basement to feed the cats before bedtime." To receive $300, what was Sandy looking for and where would be a good place to look next? Why?

For middle school aged students, history or social studies questions from chapters they are responsible for reading can be used. Usually there are review questions at the end of chapters. It is also easy enough to select questions from chapter headings or highlighted words within the chapters.

Goal Setting

The importance of goal setting is often overlooked when dealing with underachievers. If goals are set at all, they are usually focused on short term objectives and ignore long range plans. No thought is given to motivating students by pointing out real connections between the choices they are making today and the opportunities that will be available to them in the future.

In chapter two there were comparisons made between the success oriented students and underachievers. When one examines highly successful people from a wide variety of fields, they have similar characteristics. One of the things these highly achieving individuals tend to have in common is their reliance on goal setting. They tend to prefer moderately risky goals as opposed to very easy or very difficult goals. The underachievers, who at times appear to be programmed to fail, are very much the opposite. They tend to set overly ambitious goals or very simple goals. When they do succeed at these easy goals, it affords them no increase in self-worth as the goal was perceived as being so easy that anyone could have accomplished it. When they attempt to reach an unrealistically high goal and fail, they criticize themselves mercilessly for their failure.

A majority of success oriented individuals set goals often and refer to these goals on a regular basis to remind themselves of their intentions. Underachievers do not generally rely on goals as they do not enjoy the mild anxiety that goal setting produces. They do not do well under pressure and goal setting only increases pressure while achievers use this pressure as a motivator.

The most effective goals are specific and measurable. "Doing better in school" is too vague. How can such a goal be measured? It is much better to have a specific goal such as "raising my grade in math from D to B—or better." It is also a good idea to write the goal and place copies in numerous locations as a reminder. Keeping a copy in the locker, on the mirror in the student's room, and on the refrigerator makes it pretty hard to ignore.

When a student is making an initial attempt at goal setting it is a good idea to have one or two major short term goals but to also have a long term goal that is related to the successful completion of the short term goals. For example, a short term goal for an eighth grade student might be to improve his or her grades in math from D to C in order to be eligible to participate in track in the spring. Another goal may be to move into the top ten percent of the graduating class to assure a legitimate chance at winning academic scholarships. Many underachievers are so tempted by the immediate pay off they don't think about the consequences they will be faced with in the future. "Certainly it would be nice to go to the movies tonight but if I don't improve my math grade I won't be able to run track in the spring." As stated earlier, the ability to delay gratification is highly related to overall success in life.

When I was a senior in high school, I set a goal of holding a Ph.D. in psychology by the time I was thirty. I must admit I did not meet this goal. I was about seven months past my thirtieth birthday when I finished my degree. I can not say that without setting a goal I would not be completing my Ph.D., but I do believe it served as a successful motivator. There is something to be said for working toward a significant goal and the feelings that accompany reaching that goal. It makes success that much more enjoyable.

So what is to be done if the student sets goals and fails to reach them? They can pick a new goal or set the same goal until they do reach it. **Setting a goal is a successful venture if, by setting the goal, the student moved closer to reaching it than he or she would have been had it not been set.** Failing to reach a goal does not prove a student is stupid or a failure much the same way as reaching the goal does not prove the student is brilliant or a success. It merely means a student might have to work harder next time. This inappropriate overgeneralization is often at the core of the underachiever's fear. If students can be helped to see that failing to reach goals is not a black mark on their overall personhood, they will be better able to overcome the anxiety that has kept them from reaching their potential in the first place.

TEN
Counseling the Underachiever

There has been a proliferation of counseling programs associated with schools over the past couple of decades. In the past, guidance counselors focused their time and attention on providing information on career opportunities, financial aid, and academic requirements for admission into colleges and universities. The shift from academic career counseling toward psychological counseling has resulted from the overwhelming need for such services that simply weren't being provided outside of schools. There were ever increasing numbers of troubled students who wanted and needed more from counselors than help scheduling classes. Support groups began being offered in schools to address some of the more commonly occurring problems.

Student Assistance Programs

Two years ago in the district where I am currently employed, the school social worker and I were directed to start a Student Assistance Program (SAP). While there had been some support groups in the past at different buildings within the district, there had never before been a coordinated K–12 SAP program.

She and I decided we would go into the high school English classes to explain this new program. Since we were both new to the district and were describing a counseling program, we were concerned that we would meet with reluctance on the part of the students. I remember saying to her that if we could just get 20 to 25 students to sign up, we could start a few support groups and hope that word of mouth would allow us to expand the program at a later date. Much to our surprise, over 100 students wanted to participate in the SAP program. The need for counseling services was intense even in this small town in rural Wisconsin. It was like a garden that needed watering. The "flowers" had been ignored for so long they had been withering.

The most commonly offered support groups in schools tend to be in the areas of greatest need as perceived by the district's coordinators. Your district may not offer all of these groups or they may offer many more. It is also important to realize that these groups can have a host of different names but usually address the same central issues.

Families Groups

With one out of every two marriages ending in divorce, there are obviously a great many students adjusting to new family constellations at any given time. These groups are designed to help students deal with the stress and difficulties associated with changing families.

Children of Alcoholics

Research suggests that in a typical class of 25 students,

there are 4–6 students living with a chemically dependent adult. Many of these children are emotionally traumatized by the inappropriate behavior of the alcoholic. The strain that is placed upon the family can have many negative effects as well. These groups attempt to teach children the four "C's:" 1) You didn't **Cause** it. 2) You can't **Control** it. 3) You can't **Cure** it. 4) You can **Cope**.

Grief/Loss Groups

The goal of these groups is to provide support to students who have lost significant others.

Substance Abuse Groups

Some of these groups are a type of aftercare for students who have been through treatment for drug or alcohol addiction. Others have as their focus the presentation of information about the effects of alcohol and drugs on the mind and body.

It is my belief that an Underachiever/At-Risk group should be part of the support group programming in any district. If you are concerned about a son or daughter rest assured that you aren't alone. When one considers the high number of students who are at risk of failing academically and the tens of thousands of students who drop out each year it is my belief that groups for underachievers could be an effective means of supporting these students. There is not one school in this country that does not struggle with unmotivated, unsuccessful, and underachieving students. Your job as a parent is to get the ball moving in your local district. Contact the district's SAP director and ask about the possibility of starting an Underachiever/At-risk group.

One of the reasons I think it would be a good idea to serve these students in groups has to do with the feasibility of providing individual counseling to all underachieving students. There simply aren't enough counselors (or hours in the day!) However, numbers aren't my only reason for serving these students in a support group format. There are dynamics in a group that can be powerful. The simple fact that in a group setting students can learn that others share similar frustrations and disappointments can be beneficial. As group members develop feelings of closeness and trust, they can encourage each other to give up previously relied upon manipulative patterns and adopt new methods of coping with school related problems.

As stated in an earlier chapter, underachievers almost seem programmed to fail. Their negative self-concepts as learners cause feeling of anxiety when they are on the verge of success. Often they "trip themselves up" in order to keep reality in line with their perceptions of themselves as failures. Group members can encourage each other and be an effective means of countering this type of self-defeating behavior. Group members can apply positive peer pressure which is usually much more effective than influence from an adult. Remember, these group members are their friends. Kids may not be concerned about letting down a teacher or parent but they do not want to look bad in front of their peers.

Students can often times share techniques they've learned to use to deal with approaching deadlines, low motivation, negative attitudes, and other problems they might encounter. For example, Melinda only allows herself to watch television after she has completed her homework. Lyn has learned that taking notes over an important chapter really helps her retain the information and saves time studying. Lee Ann writes down all her upcoming exams on a calendar in the kitchen as a reminder.

Structure of the Group

Some important decision regarding the nature and structure of the group need to be made from the outset. These decisions will influence the facilitation of the group and, therefore, need to be made prior to the groups first meeting.

Forced vs. Voluntary Attendance

There are points to consider in favor of both compulsory and voluntary attendance to a support group. If you require students to attend who really do not want to be involved in the group, they can seriously undermine the progress of the group. They can be behavior problems or at the very least fail to participate with any real interest. On the other hand, with voluntary attendance the students who could benefit most from the group are often missed. Those students would rather not be in a situation where their behavior and choices will be examined so intensely.

My suggestion for districts considering starting such a program is to keep the participation voluntary but give the students a major incentive to attend the group. For example, they can either attend the group or serve noon hour detentions due to late or missing assignments. Given such an option most students will choose the group.

It is a good idea to reserve the right to ask students to leave the group if they are choosing to act inappropriately. It needs to be made clear to the students that simply showing up is not enough, they also need to participate in the group activities. It is possible to invite the student back into group at a later time if they express an interest and agree to change their behavior. There is a need for clear expectations regarding their behavior in the group. At the very least group members should be expected to:

1) Attend meetings regularly
2) Be on time
3) Be honest
4) Be willing to try new behaviors (i.e. take some risks)

I also think it is important for the group members to know that what is said in group stays in group. Confidentiality is important because without it there would be very little trust. Without trust there will be even less honesty.

What follows is a week by week curricula for a support group with underachieving and at-risk students. These plans are somewhat general because I believe that each counselor/

teacher needs to adapt lessons to suit their own comfort level. Use these plans as an outline to be adjusted as the group progresses.

Week 1

In the initial meeting of the group most of the time is spent going over group rules and expectations. I recommend having the group establish their own rules as it is their group designed for their benefit. It is surprising how often the students' list of rules comes very close to the rules adults would have instituted themselves.

However, it may be necessary to suggest an important rule such as confidentiality. It is vital that students understand that "what is said in group, stays in group!"

A technique I use in almost every group I run is called "Rate Your Week." Each student rates the week from 1-10 with one being very poor and ten being very good. They then explain why the week was a seven or a four. During early sessions of the group it is important for everyone to hear his or her voice in the room which breaks the ice for shy students. "Rate Your Week" is a nice way to get everyone involved and most students enjoy telling about their week.

The rest of the time during week 1 can be spent doing introductory activities. An early activity is dividing the group into pairs and each dyad spending two to three minutes telling the other group member about special hobbies or interests. The partners then switch roles so the listener becomes the speaker. The group then comes back together into a large group and each member then introduces his or her partner to the other group members. Partners can then be rotated until each member has been paired up with each group member.

There are several other non-threatening activities designed to allow group members to get to know each other.

1) Have each member tell about their favorite animal. Why is this animal your favorite animal?

2) Have students tell who they would most like to meet and why.

3) Have students tell what time in history they would like to live in if they had a choice and why.

Week 2

1) Rate Your Week

2) Quick review of group rules—It is not a bad idea to make a chart of the group rules and hang the chart somewhere in the room where the group meets as a reminder.

During week 2 it is appropriate to discuss the student's goals for both the group experience and for their academic career. The goals should be as specific as possible. It may help to ask the students to state two things they would like to learn through this group experience or name two things they would like to improve about their school performance. Have the students write these goals and turn one copy into the group leader(s) for periodic review. Each should also keep a copy to refer to daily. I also think it is a good idea to get the students to focus on their long term goals. What would they like to be doing ten years from now? A majority will respond, "I don't know."

Ask them to pretend their king of the world and have the power to make their wishes realities. If they could be doing anything they wanted, what would it be? This type of information can tell you a great deal about the student's values and what might be motivational.

An important assignment is for students to teach the group a new skill of some type. It can be whatever skill or activity they choose but should take no more than five minutes. The purpose of this exercise is to allow the students to engage in new behaviors. Hopefully this activity will produce mild feelings of discomfort in the students which they will tolerate. By learning to tolerate uncomfortable feelings they will hopefully learn to generalize this new learning into classroom situations as well. Basically, the student's learn that being uncomfortable will not kill them. They CAN stand frustration or embarrassment even if they don't like it.

As an additional motivator to get them to make certain they will participate in this activity tell the group that anyone who does not take part will have to sing a song in front of the group. This usually terrifies them even more than teaching a new skill and virtually guarantees that they will participate in the exercise.

Week 3
1) Rate Your Week
2) Teaching New Skills Lesson
After everyone has demonstrated their new skill it is important to discuss the feelings that went along with performing this new activity. The following questions will work:
    a) How did you feel when you were learning to _____?
    b) Did you eventually start to relax?
    c) Did you eventually enjoy it?
    d) Do you ever feel like this in a classroom?
    e) When?
    f) How did you deal with those feelings?

Week 4
1) Rate Your Week
2) Quick review of last weeks activities
3) Review of progress toward goals
    a) Who has an exam or project approaching?
    b) How are you preparing?
4) Lesson on study skills
This lesson can address any number of techniques such as:
    a) SQ3R
    b) how to take good notes
    c) how to improve reading comprehension
    d) test taking strategies.
    If possible let the students choose the order in which they would like to learn about these techniques.

Week 5
    1) Rate Your Week
    2) Lesson on self-talk ("Turn it Off or Turn it Around")
    The goal of this lesson is to help students understand and

counteract their self-defeating internal dialogue. Ask for a volunteer and describe a situation such as this: "It's 7:00 P.M. and you have an important test tomorrow. Your friends are going to the mall at 7:30 P.M. You would really like to go to the mall but you know if you don't study you won't be prepared for the test. What are you thinking to yourself?"

Listen to the student describe his or her self-talk and listen for the counter productive portions such as "This is stupid" or "I can always study for the next test." The goal of this exercise is to get the students to realize that this type of self-talk is the ENEMY! When the student becomes aware of this self-talk they are to do whatever it takes to "Turn it Off or Turn it Around."

Have the group brainstorm ideas for turning it off or turning it around (into something positive). Assign one member of the group to be the recorder who writes down the suggestions. After they've compiled a list you can have the group members take turns each stating which techniques will work best. The homework assignment for the next group meeting is to practice using that technique to stop negative verbalizations.

Week 6

During this final group meeting it is a good idea to review some of the major goals of the group and for the group members individually. Did each accomplish the goals? Why or why not? If things are improving academically how can each one make certain it will continue to improve?

Last but not least I always think it is a good idea to plan to meet for a follow-up session in approximately one month. In that way the students are on their own but still have links to support services if they would like additional assistance.

ELEVEN
Professional Evaluations

I wanted to include a chapter on professional evaluations because I think this is an option that should at least be considered. The information that can be provided through an individual evaluation can be tremendously helpful. As has been stated before, it is often the case that a lot of energy is expended by parents and teachers but is focused in the wrong direction. The efforts are well intended but misdirected.

A seven-year-old girl who was in first grade was really struggling with reading. The parents had been working with the child every night and were very concerned. When they came in to express their concern to the child's teacher our child study team decided to schedule a meeting to get a better understanding of the problem. The child study team consisted of a school psychologist, learning disabilities specialist, speech therapist, reading specialist and principal. The information gathered for this meeting included the fact that this child had a history of hearing difficulties as a young child. Her parents also reported that she spoke later than her older siblings. Her teacher explained that this little girl's primary problem was sounding out and blending sounds. In the parents attempt to help they had purchased the program known as "Hooked on Phonics." As the name implies, "Hooked on Phonics" is a program that focuses on sounding out words as a key to reading success. The program may be excellent for some students but it was not working for this child. As I suspected, this child had what is known as an auditory discrimination problem. She could not hear the subtle differences between similar sounding words. Due to this difficulty, sounding out words would be a very difficult skill for her to master. "Hooked on Phonics" had the child focusing on her weakest skills area rather than looking for a strength to build upon. This is a classic example of well intended efforts resulting in poor results. Not only was the child not learning but she was becoming frustrated. The child was nearly in tears at the mention of "reading."

An evaluation typically involves several highly trained professionals administering a battery of tests, conducting observations, and gathering other data regarding a child's skills. The tests include measures of a child's intellectual functioning (the aforementioned IQ test) as well as their current skills in subject areas such as reading, math, spelling and written language. Many times the tests also include measures of:

—receptive language (how well a child understands what is spoken)

—expressive language (how well they produce language)

—visual-motor integration (how well they can "see" a design and then recreate or draw it)

—psychological measures such as measures of personality, achievement orientation, and frustration tolerance.

All public schools have to provide evaluation services free of charge upon request. Some schools districts aren't very enthused about evaluating a child at the request of the parents but don't let your school district discourage you by seeming too busy or by down playing your child's problems. It is your tax dollars paying for these services. Simply explain you'd like this evaluation to determine if there is anything that is not being done for the student that could be beneficial. Most schools will be more than happy to provide this service especially if they believe you are sincerely ready to help with the child's education.

Why go to the trouble of getting an evaluation? As already has been mentioned, time and energy are precious commodities today. It seems that everyone (even children) are more and more pressed for time. It only makes sense if you are going to invest an hour a night with your child's academics you might as well make every effort to make certain that the hour can provide the maximum results. A comprehensive evaluation is an excellent way to gather information about virtually all factors that influence a child's learning. Before attempts are made to set up behavioral contracts and study schedules, it is a good idea to make certain that the child can see and hear. I've seen many instances where 90% of the difficulty in school has been something as simple as the child not being able to see the black board.

Also, by allowing other professionals to use their knowledge and skills regarding the learning process, they might pick up on something that is occurring that the classroom teacher is missing. Imagine the classroom teacher trying to see to the individual needs of 25 to 35 second graders. It is very easy to understand how a teacher can miss something important while other professional have the luxury of focusing on one child at a time.

When I observe a classroom one of the things I look for is whether or not a child is "on task" a higher percentage of time when the teacher is within a few feet of the student. This is often the case with underachievers. Once a teacher is aware that Jimmy is on task 85% of the time when the teacher is within six feet of him and on task only 27% of the time when the teacher is farther away, the teacher can either consciously spend more time in that student's area or simply move the child to a location where most of the instructing is done.

Another reason to have an evaluation is to receive recommendations on how to help at home. As has been stressed throughout this book, a coordinated effort between home and school is the best approach. The classroom teacher can provide missed assignments to be made up, the reading specialist can give specific remedial techniques, and the psychologist can suggest ideas to help motivate the student.

Perhaps the most important reason to request an evaluation is to determine what weaknesses are keeping the child from achieving full potential. Are there weaknesses that require remediation? If a pattern of underachievement is long standing, there will undoubtedly be "holes" in the child's learning. For example, the student may be only a year behind in math skills in general, but has virtually no skills when it comes to fractions. Another example may be that the student reads words at grade level but comprehends what he has read three years below grade level. This type of specific information helps parents determine what areas to concentrate on while working with the student.

After the evaluation has been completed, I recommend that students be involved in the meeting once they reach an age where they can comprehend this information. Unfortunately I can't give you a hard and fast rule regarding when a student should attend these meetings. At the very least the parents can sit down with the child and explain the results of the evaluation later at home. If the student has a weakness in a particular area, he or she needs to be aware of this weakness. The student also needs to hear about techniques that will help with compensation.

This is also the time when students can learn about their dominant learning style. If they do have a weakness or a strength in a particular area, they are the ones who have to live with this situation. If, for example, a student is a visual learner and has a poor memory, the importance of getting an assignment notebook can be stressed. At the same time parents can be told to give commands one at a time. If you tell this child,

"I want you to go to your room, get your white clothes that need washing, and put them in the hamper in my room," the child may get to the room and remember something about clothes but there is little or no chance of remembering the entire request. These commands need to be given in a manner that takes into consideration that the student has difficulties with memory. In this example the commands could be broken down into smaller segments.

Last, but not least, a child may not be an underachiever at all. The student may be earning "C's" which are realistic for this student. Not every student is destined to be an academic star even if the siblings are straight "A" students. An evaluation will at the very least give parents an idea of reasonable expectations for their child.

During an evaluation one of the questions that can be answered is whether or not a child is functioning with a **learning disability (LD)** or **emotional disability (ED)**. In some states ED is actually called a **behavioral disability (BD).** There are other disabilities as well such as mental retardation, speech/ language disabled, or physically handicapped but LD and ED are by far the most commonly occurring disability.

The definition of what constitutes a learning disability differs from state to state. Most definitions include compli- cated formulas that rely on a statistical technique known as regression analysis. I'll spare you a discussion of regression analysis because in reality the formulas that are used have more to do with the amount of money a state is willing to spend on a student than with any relevant educational issues.

To be diagnosed as learning disabled they must demon- strate at least average intelligence (i.e. in most states this means an IQ of 85 and above.) Most definitions also contain some requirement of "processing deficits" which means the student has difficulties processing or conceptualizing infor- mation. It may be that this processing deficit manifests itself through visual, auditory, or kinesthetic channels. The key factor in determining whether or not a student qualifies as learning disabled has to do with their current level of achievement as it relates to their overall potential. For a student to be diagnosed as learning disabled there must be a "significant discrepancy" between his or her potential (as measured by an intelligence test) and his or her current academic performance. This means that if a student has an IQ score of 100 (average ability), performing academically at that same level is to be expected (i.e. approximately at grade level.) If there is a difference between what is expected and what is actually occurring, a discrepancy exists. It still needs to be determined if there is a "significant discrepancy" which means, "Are they far enough behind?" Once again, each state is different in policies and guidelines. In some states, students two or more years behind their current grade placement are considered to be functioning with a significant discrepancy between what is expected and what is occurring.

In Wisconsin, a mathematical formula is used to determine who qualifies and who does not. A student's IQ is multiplied by the number of years they have been in school. The student then must be 50% behind that figure to qualify.

IQ 100
6th grade completed = 7 years of school
50% behind
3.5 grade level

In the above example a sixth grade student with an IQ score of 100 must be scoring at or below the third grade, fifth month level to qualify as learning disabled. If you're not confused yet I'd be impressed!

Many times a student is found to be behind his or her classmates but not far enough behind. However, there is obviously a problem because the student is behind his or her classmates. It is not legal to provide specialized support services until the student falls even further behind and the family is really at their wits end. Many times this is a frustrating situation for the student, the family, and the school.

As has been mentioned earlier, many times underachievers are masters of manipulation. They can be very convincing in the role of the "struggling student" when their real motivation is to involve the parents or teachers to such an extent that their academic difficulties become another's problem. How can a parent or teacher know if a student is having true academic difficulties or is just depending on them to help complete their work? Sylvia Rimm (1990) has written a number of books on academic difficulties and lists several means of distinguishing between the dependent student and the disabled student.

Dependence	**Disability**
1. Child asks for explanations regularly despite differences in the subject matter.	Child asks for explanations in particular subjects which are difficult.
2. Child asks for explanations of instructions regardless of style used, either auditory or visual.	Child asks for explanation of instructions only when given in one instructional style, either auditory or visual, but not both.
3. Child's questions are not specific to material but appear to be mainly to gain adult attention.	Child's questions are specific to material and once the process is explained the child works efficiently.
4. Child is disorganized or slow in assignments but becomes much more efficient when a meaningful reward is presented as motivation.	Child's disorganization or slow pace continues despite motivating rewards.
5. Child works only when an adult is nearby at school and/or at home.	Child works independently once process is clearly explained.
6. Individually administered measures of ability indicate	Both individual and group measures indicate lack of

that the child is capable of learning the material. Individual test improve with tester encouragement and support. Group measures may not indicate good abilities or skills.

specific abilities or skills. Tester encouragement has no significant effect on scores.

7. Child exhibits "poor me" language (tears, helplessness, pouting, copying) regularly when new work is presented. Teacher or adult attention serves to ease the symptoms.

Child exhibits "poor me" body language only with instructions or assignments in specific disability areas and accepts challenges in areas of strength.

8. Parents report whining, complaining, attention getting, temper tantrums, and poor sportsmanship at home.

Although parents may find similar symptoms at home, they tend to be more sporadic than regular, particularly the whining and complaining.

9. Child's "poor me" behavior appears only with one parent and not with the other; only with some teachers and not with others. With some teachers or with other parent the child functions fairly well independently.

Although the child's "poor me" behaviors may only appear with one parent or with solicitous teachers, performance is not adequate even when behavior is acceptable.

10. Child learns only when given one-to-one instruction but will not learn in groups even when instructional mode is varied.

Although child may learn more quickly in one-to-one setting, he/she will also learn efficiently in a group setting provided the child's disability is taken into consideration when instructions are given.

(Rimm, 1990, p. 169-170)

Defining what makes up an emotional disability (ED) is perhaps even more confusing. Like LD, the definitions for ED change from state to state. Unlike LD, it has no convenient mathematical formula and many times determining who qualifies for special educational support as ED is very much a subjective determination.

In general, a good rule in determining whether or not a student is suffering from an emotional disability can be answered by addressing the simple question "Is the student's emotional state interfering with his or her ability to learn?" More specific questions to be addressed are as follows:

"Are they acting in an appropriate manner with their peers and teachers?"

"Are they suffering from depression or having physical symptoms due to stress or anxiety?"

"Are they acting in an inappropriate manner under what could be considered normal circumstances?"

As you can see, these questions are not easily answered and there may be a good deal of disagreement between the various professionals who evaluated the child.

As the parents of the child being evaluated, it is important to remember that you are in control of the evaluation. The school needs your written permission to conduct the evaluation. If you are unhappy with the evaluation, at any point in the process you can revoke that consent. If at the end of the process, your child qualified for special educational assistance, you have the right to deny placement. If you decide to agree to a placement in a special classroom for a trial period, you can always change your mind and have your child returned to the regular classroom. The school still must honor YOUR request for a comprehensive evaluation but as the parent you are in control of the evaluation.

The Pros and Cons of Special Education

There are both positive and negative aspects of LD and ED programs. Careful consideration must be given by both parents and educators before a student is placed in such a program.

On the positive side, there are smaller numbers of students in such classrooms. It is not uncommon for a special education class to have only five to seven students for one full time teacher. Therefore, the children receive a lot of individual instruction. They can receive the kind of attention it typically takes to remediate a learning problem.

It is important never to lose sight of the fact that learning disabled children in all likelihood won't learn at the same rate as other students. They may have significant memory problems, organizational difficulties, and a host of other deficits that makes learning harder for them. In a classroom of 25-35 students, they will be expected to sink or swim. In a classroom of five, individual needs can be focused upon. Distractions are kept to a minimum in smaller classrooms. The students receive direct instruction and immediate feedback on their performances.

In a special classroom they will be instructed by teachers who have had specialized training in working with students who have disabilities. They have undoubtedly worked with students who have had similar disabilities in the past and may be able to provide higher quality instruction to the student.

Another piece of information to consider is once a student has been identified as having a disability they will probably be promoted to the next grade. It is some what of an unwritten rule that special educational students are not retained. Once teachers understand a student has a disability, they will often grade a student with more of an eye on the effort the student puts forth than on the quality of the work. Not all teachers are that considerate but, in general, this tends to be true.

Some may think that by lowering expectations for a student we allow students to continue to slide by. It's important to realize that in this section of the book we are proceeding with the assumption that the student has a real disability and is not simply choosing not to perform successfully. I do not feel it is a mistake to lower expectations as long as the expectations are in line with the student's abilities. To expect a ninth grader who is reading at a fourth grade level to meet the same expectations as his or her classmates is unfair. However, to expect an underachieving ninth grader who has the ability to perform at grade level but is choosing not to perform to be held to the same standards as his or her classmates is totally appropriate.

It is a reality though that most teachers will expect less from a special education student. There is much research to show that teacher expectations do influence student performance. Teachers may not call on an LD child as often. They may not wait as long for a response from an LD child. Teachers may even grade the students work lower simply because they know the child has a learning disability. All of these factors need to be considered when trying to decide whether or not special education would be a benefit to the child.

There are other negative factors associated with being diagnosed with a disability. The most obvious one is having to do with carrying a label that ends with "disability." These children can be stigmatized by this label and can be teased by their classmates. They are required to go to that "special room" with the "dummies."

It is wise to consider how the child might react to this. Will they hate the program and purposefully be a royal pain trying to get out? Or are they so tired of struggling and failing that going to a place where they are taught at a more appropriate level would be a welcome relief? If a child is dead set against such assistance, the program is not likely to be successful. If they are willing to receive help with their academic or emotional needs, it can be very helpful.

Another negative associated with special education is that in many ways it is like a "black hole." The children go in but they don't come out. My best guess is that over 90% of special education students never leave the program even though that is the goal. Once they are placed in the program they get used to the individual instruction. To be placed back into the regular education environment would be too much and they wouldn't be successful.

Many times special education can set up another self-fulfilling prophecy. Students believe they are incapable of being successful and it is this belief, more than any academic deficit, that keeps them from achieving. Think of an example in your own life where you found yourself saying, "I can't do this. This is much too difficult." Did you persevere and succeed or did you give up and fail?

Another concern regarding special education is that this population of students has a higher drop out rate than other groups. Whether or not placement in special education causes these students to drop out is open to debate because an argument can also be made that they are less successful and would be more likely to drop out with or without special education. The fact remains more special education students fail to receive a diploma than regular education students.

Finally, attention needs to be paid to the individual program your child will be attending. Will the child receive intense remediation of their academic deficiencies or will they simply be taught at a lower grade level? If attempts are not being made to improve their weaknesses then they are obviously not in an optimal program. Don't be afraid to ask for names of parents who have students in the program. The school may explain that that information is confidential. Ask if the school would be willing to have parents of children already in such programs call you which would not break confidentiality. These parents are an excellent source of information but please don't talk to just one. Get several different opinions before making up your mind.

TWELVE
Other Considerations

At this point let's assume that as a parent or teacher you have followed the suggestions in the book. You've taken the time and trouble to contact the schools to try and monitor the student's progress on a regular basis. Let's also assume that the professionals at the school have been cooperative and shared information regarding their recommendations to help the student. You have set up clear expectations and administered reasonable consequences in accordance with the student's behavior. You may have tried tutoring the student directly or hired tutorial assistance. Let's also assume things are still going poorly. There are some additional factors that could possibly explain why a student is still struggling.

Drug Use
As frightening as the thought of drug use can be to parents,

it had better be considered as a potential contributing factor in academic difficulties. Drug use can have an effect on numerous components that are directly related to school success such as concentration, motivation, and persistence. There are too many cases of adults "looking the other way" because they are afraid to ask the hard questions. Actually it is not the questions they are afraid of; it's the answers. The attitude that exists in so many homes seems to be that ignoring the problem will solve it. Things usually don't work that way and ignoring some situations may actually exacerbate the problem by sending the student the message that: 1) "We know you are using drugs and don't care" or: 2) "What you do with your mind and body is your business."

Within a family each individual should be given personal space and freedom to find themselves and discover their own identity. Adolescence is a time to try various roles and experiment at this business called "life." I do not believe that freedom can include experimenting with life threatening behaviors such as using drugs. Teenagers are still considered "minors" and with good reason. They simply have not had the life experience to know what is in their best interests.

The reason drug use or abuse needs to be considered in cases of underachievement is that one of the first tell tale signs of drug use is falling grades. Adolescents who were formerly solid students but are now missing assignments and failing a majority of classes are suspect. Other warning signs are:

1) **Change in peer groups**—Is the child now spending a majority of their time with a new set of friends? Are these new friends the type of friends that you may not approve of? If this is the case you might consider calling the school guidance counselor, psychologist, or assistant principal and openly asking, "Are my son/daughter's friends suspected of being drug users?" They may not be able or willing to answer that question but one thing is certain, if the general consensus at school is that this group of students are believed to be using drugs , you can be quite confident that they ARE using drugs.

2) **Change in temperament**—Has your normally happy-

go-lucky child become subdued and moody? Does the child feel "awful" on weekend mornings? Does he or she "fly off the handle" at the slightest disappointment or inconvenience? A moody teenager is not uncommon, but be concerned when these factors are more pronounced than usual.

3) **Unexplained absences** — Are there missed school days on Mondays and Fridays? I've worked with many teenage alcoholics and addicts and a majority fit this pattern of Monday/Friday absences. Friday is missed to start partying early and Monday is recuperation time. Is the student tardy the first period after lunch? This is often a sign that they are drinking or using over the lunch hour.

The following is a brief description of the most commonly abused drugs and physical symptoms associated with the use and abuse of these substances.

Alcohol

It is sad but true that many individuals still don't realize or won't accept that alcohol is a drug. In fact, it is one of the oldest drugs. Alcohol is as popular today as ever which is probably due to its social acceptability and easy access. Many parents have the attitude when they find out their child has been using alcohol, "Thank God he wasn't using drugs!" It is not uncommon for parents to let their adolescents drink in the home or with them at a restaurant.

Physical Symptoms:
- -red, blood shot eyes
- -slurred speech
- -loss of motor control
- -talkativeness
- -drowsiness
- -lack of interest in formerly rewarding activities

Cocaine or Crack

Cocaine use appears to be declining among high school students but is still a major problem for several reasons: 1) Both cocaine and crack (which is a crystallized form of cocaine) are extremely addictive with one in every four individuals who use these drugs becoming addicted and 2) Crack is very inexpensive and easy to obtain.

According to a study conducted by researchers associated with the Cocaine Hotline, one out of six teenagers graduating from high school has tried cocaine. The results of this study clearly demonstrate the addictive power of cocaine. Over half of the callers felt addicted to cocaine (61%), could not limit their use (73%), and could not refuse cocaine when it was available (83%). Two-thirds (67%) said they were unable to abstain from using the drug for one month. They preferred cocaine to food (71%), sex (50%), and family activities (76%).

Physical Symptoms:
- -chronic depression
- -irritability
- -difficulties sleeping
- -running noses
- -bloody noses
- -chronic fatigue
- -periodic hyperness

Marijuana

Another common misconception is that marijuana is not addictive. WRONG! Individuals can become psychologically addicted to marijuana in much the same way as they become addicted to any substance. Once individuals believe they *must* have something to get by or survive, they are addicted. The marijuana of today is ten times more potent than in the 1960s and '70s. One in four Americans have now tried marijuana and one in 12 use it on a regular basis. Be on the look out for a sickly sweet odor in the bedroom or on the clothes. Also, keep an eye out for seeds or leaves in the pockets of their clothes, or rolling papers or pipes.

Physical Symptoms:
- -red eyes and constant use of eye drops
- -binge eating or "intense munchies"

-hysterical laughter over mildly amusing situations (i.e. laughter that is exaggerated in its chronicity and intensity)

Stimulants
Stimulants have chemical properties that speed up the actions of the central nervous system. Amphetamines are the most commonly used stimulants and have slang terms such as speed, crank, crystal, uppers, bennies, go-fast, and meth.
Physical Symptoms:
  -loss of appetite
  -excessive talkativeness
  -trembling hands
  -enlarged pupils
  -lack of sleep
  -excessive perspiration

Depressants
Depressants slow down the body and are often prescribed by doctors for legitimate medical treatments. However, that does not mean these drugs can not be abused. Some of the more commonly prescribed depressants are Valium, Nembutal, and Seconal. They are commonly referred to as "downers" on the street.
Physical Symptoms:
  -drowsiness
  -slurred speech
  -slowed body movements
  -depression
  -physical awkwardness or clumsiness

A final point that is worth mentioning, if you find drug paraphernalia, concrete steps should be taken to have a drug and alcohol assessment of your child. When confronted expect that the student will tell you things like, "I found it at school," or "I'm holding it for a friend, but I never use drugs" etc. **Don't let your fear paralyze you.** If you find rolling papers (usually the brand name is Zig Zags), a pipe, or a water pipe (i.e. a bong), it is even more apparent that an assessment or blood test is necessary.

Depression

In an article appearing in the December 2, 1992 edition of *USA Today* it was reported that depression in America has been increasing with each passing generation since records started being kept. In this longitudinal study the researchers reported that depression is "nearing epidemic proportions." Having worked with school aged students I have no difficulties believing the accuracy of the last statement. As part of a research project I completed recently the Beck Depression Inventory (BDI) was administered to eighty (80) high school students and twenty-five scored in a range that would indicate the presence of at least mild depression. The results of this study indicated that 31% (almost one out of three) students who were selected at random from a rural, Midwestern high school responded that they at times felt at least mildly to moderately depressed.

The reason I am discussing depression in a book about underachievement is that rapidly falling grades can be a "red flag" that something more serious than academic difficulties may be occurring. Falling grades can be an indicator of depression and/or other psychological disturbances. A student who is depressed often times lacks the energy to complete assignments. Students simply don't care one way or the other about things such as grades when they are struggling with depression.

There are physical causes of depression that are related to chemical imbalances in the brain but a majority of cases are caused by an individual's attitudes and perceptions. As has been pointed out throughout this book, feelings are not caused by events, but by the views people take of these events. **People feel how they think.**

The cognitive psychologist Aaron Beck (1977) postulated three primary beliefs which he called the **cognitive triad** that lead to depression. These three beliefs have at their core 1) **a** negative view of the self, 2) **a negative view of the world,** and 3) **a negative view of the future**. Common expressions that accompany these beliefs are:

1. Negative View of the Self

   "I'm a no good piece of garbage."

   "I can't do anything right (therefore I'm totally worthless)."

   "I'll never be good enough."

2. Negative View of the World

   "Life sucks!"

   "The world is an awful place."

   "Life is too hard. It's horrible."

3. Negative View of the future

   "It'll only get worse."

   "Things won't ever get any better than they are right now."

   "The world is so screwed up, it's going to end." (Wilde, 1992, p. 56-57.)

Symptoms of Depression:

   -irritability

   -crying easily and often

   -loss of interest in activities previously pleasurable

   -excessive guilt

   -feelings of hopelessness

   -references to suicide (i.e. "No one would care if I killed myself.")

   -interest in death (i.e. reading books and poetry on death, images of death)

   -decrease in physical activity

   -loss of energy

   -change in sleep patterns, either waking up early and being unable to get back to sleep or wanting to sleep all the time

   -loss of weight

   -loss of interest in sex

   -giving away prized possessions

Children and adolescents who have experienced a

significant loss may also exhibit some of the aforementioned symptoms. The death of a significant other, change in the family structure, divorce, loss of a favorite pet, change in schools, or other changes in the child's life can bring about what is called reactive depression. As the name suggestions, the depression is viewed as a reaction to the change in the student's environment.

It is worth mentioning that while a majority of these symptoms appear to pertain to adolescents, it is quite possible for younger children to be depressed. Several years ago, I had a seven-year-old referred to me because he had been hitting his infant sister. It turned out that the boy was severely depressed and suicidal. Yes, you read that correctly; a suicidal seven-year-old.

Small children can suffer from depression the same way adults suffer from depression. It is more common for small children who are depressed to exhibit feelings of anger and rage when they are depressed. That is not to say they also don't exhibit classic symptoms of depression such as extreme sadness and irritability. The point is that an acting out, angry seven-year-old very well may also be a depressed seven-year-old.

If your child or student is experiencing some of the above mentioned symptoms he or she may be suffering from depression. *Please seek professional help.* This is not something to take lightly. It is too important to take chances.

THIRTEEN
Walking Away

Before you jump to conclusions about the title of this chapter, note that the title is "Walking Away," not "Giving Up." There is a big difference between the two. The title is intended to remind readers that there may come a time when the kindest thing a parent or teacher can do is allow the natural consequences of a child's choices to hit home at full impact. Sometimes the only way people learn is through the pain of their mistakes.

There may come a time when parents and teachers feel like they've honestly done everything in their power to help students be successful and they have rejected all of these efforts. As the saying goes, "You can lead a horse to water, but you can't make it drink." With an underachiever the saying can be slightly modified to, "You can provide students with opportunities to be successful, but you can't take their exams (or turn in their homework.)" If they are choosing to be irresponsible and behave in ways that will lead to failure, they will probably fail no matter what anyone does.

Occasionally parents become so adept at "rescuing" their child that he or she begins to rely upon the parent to always pick up the pieces. If the parent can somehow break this pattern and allow the student to fall right smack on his/her nose for the first time (even though it feels like the parent is the one falling), it may bring about some real changes. It may be time to give the child the opportunity to take control again and be responsible for his/her own destiny. In the final analysis, the student has got to want to succeed. All the rewards and consequences are external motivators. Some of the "juice" has to come from the inside.

There are other situations that can arise where it might be necessary to disengage. When the strain of an underachieving child starts causing significant problems in your family, marriage, and personal life, it may be time to walk away. **No individual in a family is more important than the health of the entire family**. I have seen many situations where the stress of an underachieving child causes difficulties in other areas.

The following is a story about an underachiever named Johnny. The oldest of four children, Johnny was always a "decent" student but never really "applied himself." He was more interested in athletics and usually did what was necessary to get by academically. His younger sister was a perfect 4.0 student, won numerous academic awards/scholarships, and turned out to be Valedictorian of her class.

I know the family well and I'm certain there were many discussions regarding Johnny's school work. Undoubtedly there were attempts to get Johnny to buckle down and focus on school. Anyone who spent time with Johnny could tell he was bright and it seemed like there was a lot of wasted potential. The summer after he graduated from high school his father asked him about his plans for finding a job for the summer. Johnny was looking for a job but usually after he had slept until noon. In other words, he wasn't looking very hard. He thought his family would help with finances and he wanted to take a break before beginning the hard work at college. Johnny no doubt thought, "Why not have a relaxing summer?" He would have been interested if a part time job came open, but it was apparent it was not a priority. He felt he had "earned" the summer off.

His father and mother were concerned about Johnny and his lack of motivation and thought long and hard about the situation. They finally decided to have a talk with Johnny and told him they loved him very much and nothing would ever change that. They also told him, "You're old enough to live your life any way you want. It's just that we're not going to pay for it anymore. If you decide to go away to school in the fall and you show us that you are serious about being there, then we'll talk about the family helping to pay for the spring semester. You're on your own for the fall semester. We are fully prepared if you decide not to go to school. This is very important and we want to make sure you understand exactly what we're telling you." Johnny looked up with his eyes full of tears and said, "You're cutting me off."

Within 24 hours of that conversation, Johnny had one job and eventually worked two jobs that summer. He did go to college in the fall and came home with a 3.5 GPA. His father commented that he wasn't sure Johnny could read because he had never seen him with a book prior to college! After the first semester, Johnny was accepted into an honors program and continued to work hard and do well. He took summer classes and started to enjoy the challenge that college was providing. After a career of being a "B" and "C" student, he was now consistently on the dean's list. Johnny graduated in three and a half years (a semester early) with a double major.
He found out recently that he has been accepted into several law schools. Johnny's biggest problem now is trying to decide which law school to attend.

This is a true story. Johnny is my nephew. I wanted to share this story with you to let you know that things can and do change. Here's hoping you've got a Johnny waiting to blossom at your house!

APPENDIX

The Tools of Evaluation

As an aid in helping parents and teachers understand the evaluation process, an understanding of the instruments or tests most often used by members of the evaluation team is helpful. It would also be beneficial for both parents and teachers to have a basic understanding of the psychometric properties of these tests. The numbers and statistics can be overwhelming but actually are easy to comprehend once a few simple facts about the nature of these tests are explained.

The tests discussed are referred to as **norm referenced.** This means that the author or authors of a test start by compiling a list of questions or problems they feel will measure whatever skill or ability they are trying to assess. The next step is to actually administer the test to a representative sample of students. The group of students that makes up this sample and takes the test should be representative of the country as a whole. For example, this sample should include students from different geographic regions of the country. Efforts should be made to make a close approximation regarding the proportion of various ethnic classes included in the sample. The same should be true for urban vs. rural students.

Once this data is collected the authors analyze the response patterns and select the questions they feel are the most accurate and do the best job of measuring what the authors are intending to measure. The data collected from this sample of students is also used to determine what scores are considered average as compared to low average and so on.

This is how "norming" a test works in theory anyway. Many tests are not adequately "normed" because the expense and effort involved in doing this properly can be tremendous. Be advised that "all tests are not created equally!" The tests that I am going to briefly describe are the most commonly used. If you have a question regarding a test there are several ways you can get access to information regarding the norming procedures to determine whether the instrument was normed adequately. The test manual will contain this information and you should be able to see the manual when you meet with the professionals that evaluate your student. There are also books available that review these instruments that should be available at your public library. The *Mental Measurement Yearbook* which is published by the University of Nebraska and *Psychological Measurement* by Anastasi are two excellent sources which can be located at most public libraries.

These test scores are typically reported in a number of ways that can seem confusing but actually are not as complicated as they appear. The most commonly used scores are: 1) standard scores, 2) percentiles, and 3) grade equivalencies.

A **standard score** typically has an average of 100. Standard scores are important because they allow for the meaningful comparison of scores on different tests. As the name implies, standard scores set up a standard or equal scale of measurement to allow for this comparison.

If a child received a score of 26 out of 50 on a math test and a score of 39 out of 50 on a spelling test, could it be concluded that the student did better on the spelling test than on the math test? Not necessarily. It could be that the average score on the math test was 20 (a very hard test, indeed!) and the average score on the spelling test was 45 (a real "no brainer"). The score of 26 on the math test would actually be a better score than the 39 on the spelling test, but unless these scores were turned into standard scores there would be no way of comparing the two in any meaningful way. It would be like comparing apples to oranges. With standard scores, we are comparing apples to apples.

Percentiles or **percentile ranks** are much easier to understand. A student's performance on a test will fall somewhere between the 1st and 99th percentile. Students scoring within the 20th percentile are achieving at a point where 79% of the other students scored higher. This student did as well or better than 20% of students their age who took the test.

Grade equivalencies are the scores preferred by teachers, but are often very misunderstood. What many educators believe is that a student obtaining a grade level of 5.3 is performing at a fifth grade, third month level. This is **not** correct. A grade level equivalency of 5.3 means that a student is performing like an average student who has received five years, three months of instruction. The difference between these two may not be apparent at first but consider the following example and the difference can be quite significant.

Let's say a third grade student answers every single math problem correctly on an achievement test like the Iowa Test of Basic Skills and receives a grade level equivalency of 9.3. This student could not perform ninth grade mathematics which is a mixture of algebra and arithmetic. They have not been exposed to this type of material. The 9.3 means that they are able to work with the third grade material the way an average student who has received nine years, three months of instruction would perform. It does not mean they are able to correctly work ninth grade mathematics problems.

The Weschler Instruments

There are four tests produced by David Weschler that will briefly be reviewed here. All of these instruments are intelligence tests with averages of 100 and standard deviations of 15. A standard deviation can be thought of as the average amount scores differ from the average. While that is not a precise definition it can be helpful in understanding the concept of standard deviation. Two out of three individuals fall within one standard deviation of 100. If a student falls within this range of 85—115 they are within a well populated section of the scale which contains 66.7% or 2/3 of all individuals tested.

The Weschler instruments are the most popular intelligence tests used by psychologists today. If another intelligence test is used for the student, parents and teachers should ask why. That is not to say that all other tests are invalid because there are other instruments that may do an adequate job of measuring intelligence. It's just that the Weschler instruments are so commonly used.

Weschler Intelligence Scale for Children-Revised (WISC-R, 1974)
Weschler Intelligence Scale for Children-Third Edition(WISC-III 1991)

The WISC-R and WISC-III will be reviewed together because the WISC-III is simply an updated version of the WISC-R. The WISC-III was published in 1991 but many professionals still rely on the WISC-R. The age range for the WISC-III is 6—0 to 16—11.

These tests yield three major scores:

Full Scale IQ—the total score or intelligence quotient (IQ)

Verbal IQ—which measures verbal skills

Performance IQ—which measures visual-perceptual skills

The Verbal and Performance subtests are composed of five required subtests and an optional subtest. The WISC-III performance scale has two optional subtests (Symbol Search and Mazes). Each of the subtests has an average score of 10 and a standard deviation of three. Therefore, an average score of 10 on all ten subtests will yield the Full Scale average of 100.

The following are the individual subtests:

Verbal Scale

1) **Information**—measures long term memory of acquired knowledge.

2) **Similarities**—measures abstract verbal reasoning and/or logical thinking.

3) **Arithmetic**—measures the ability to mentally manipulate mathematical operations.

4) **Vocabulary**—measures a student's vocabulary skills or general fund of information.

5) **Comprehension**—measures social judgment or social competence.

6) **Digit Span**—(optional) measures short-term auditory memory.

Performance Scale

1) **Picture Completion**—measures awareness to detail or the ability to distinguish essential from non-essential detail.

2) **Picture Arrangement**—measures the ability to anticipate the consequences of an act.

3) **Block Design**—measures perceptual organization as well as visual motor coordination.

4) **Object Assembly**—measures the ability to synthesize abstract parts into meaningful wholes.

5) **Coding**—measures rote visual learning and speed of visual processing.

6) **Symbol Search**—(optional) measures visual discrimination abilities.

7) **Mazes**—(optional) measures planning ability and perceptual organization.

Weschler Preschool and Primary Scale of Intelligence-Revised (WPPSI-R, 1989)

This instrument follows much of the same properties as it big brothers the WISC-R and WISC-III except that it is designed for children aged 3–0 to 7–3. Several of the subtests are different on the WPPSI-R. A majority of the subtests on the WPPSI-R are also contained on the WISC-R and WISC-III. Object Assembly, Block Design, Mazes. Picture Completion, Information, Comprehension, Arithmetic, Vocabulary, and Similarities are included on all three tests. The following three subtests on the WPPSI-R are unique to the test.

1) **Geometric Design**—measures perceptual recognition and hand eye coordination.

2) **Animal Pegs**—measures a student's ability to associate sign with symbols.

3) **Sentences**—measures short-term auditory memory.

Weschler Adult Intelligence Scale—Revised (WAIS-R, 1978)

The WAIS-R is simply the adult intelligence test for individuals over the age of 16. It also has an average of 100 and contains the same subtests as the WISC-R although Coding is now called Digit Symbol. Many of the questions on the WISC-R and WAIS-R are identical. Since it is doubtful that many adolescents will have any exposure to the WAIS-R, a more detailed analysis will not be presented.

Kaufman Assessment Battery for Children (K-ABC) (Kaufman and Kaufman, 1983)

The K-ABC is an intelligence test that has been gaining in popularity over the past decade and has probably overtaken some of the previously relied upon instruments to become the second most commonly used intelligence test. It is intended for use with children 2 years, 6 months to 12 years, 5 months. It requires approximately the same amount of time to administer as the Weschler instrument (approximately one hour). The K-ABC also has an average of 100 and a standard deviation of 15 like the Weschler intelligence tests.

Unlike the Weschlers which break down into Verbal and Performance Scales, the K-ABC divides into four scales:

Sequential Processing—measures a child's ability to solve problems that require the arrangement of material into a sequential or serial order.

Simultaneous Processing—measures a child's ability to solve problems that require the processing of many stimuli at once.

Achievement Scale—measures factual knowledge and academic skills such as reading, arithmetic, and vocabulary.

Non-Verbal Scale—measures a child's ability to solve problems that do not require a verbal response.

There are ten subtests that make up what is called the **Mental Processing Composite** (which is the equivalent of the Weschler IQ). There are six subtests that make up the **Achievement Scale**.

1) **Magic Window**—measures the ability to pay close attention to detail and the ability to distinguish essential from non-essential detail.

2) **Face Recognition**—measures short-term visual memory and the ability to use successful scanning strategies.

3) **Hand Movement**—measures motor reproduction of a sequence as well as short term visual memory.

4) **Gestalt Closure**—measures a child's ability to "pull together" or integrate parts into a whole.

5) **Number Recall**—measures short-term auditory memory.

6) **Triangles**—measures visual motor problem solving.

7) **Word Order**—measures a child's ability to integrate auditory and visual skills on the same task.

8) **Matrix analogies**—measures a child's visual reasoning skills.

9) **Spatial memory**—measures short-term visual memory.

10) **Photo Series**—measures a child's ability to judge the consequences of an act or basic cause and effect relationships.

The K-ABC has been criticized as under representing

minority populations when the instrument was normed. It is reported that Hispanic-Americans are under represented by 24% and that low education level blacks were under represented by 10%.

The following instruments are what are known as achievement instruments. They are not measures of intelligence but rather measures of a student's performance in areas such as reading, mathematics, spelling, and written language.

Wide Range Achievement Test—Revised (WRAT-R) (Jastak and Wilkinson, 1984)

The WRAT-R is a very commonly used achievement test which is unfortunate because this test is not one of the better instruments available. The WRAT-R measures reading, mathematics, and spelling. It divides into Level I (five years to 11 years, 11 months) and Level II (12 years to 74 years, 11 months).

The problem with the WRAT-R is that it is a very short instrument and requires only 30—40 minutes to administer which is one of the reasons for its popularity. It is often described as "the quick and dirty test." The WRAT-R would be best if used as a screening instrument and not as a measure of actual academic skill acquisition. There simply aren't enough questions to do an adequate job of measuring the various subject areas. Missing two or three problems in mathematics can make a significant change in the student's score. The Reading section is actually a measure of a student's ability to pronounce words and does measure reading comprehension.

Kaufman Test of Educational Achievement (K-TEA) (Kaufman and Kaufman, 1985)

The K-TEA is intended for ages 6-18 and requires approximately one hour to administer. It includes the following four subtests:

Reading Decoding—(60 items) measures a child's ability to identify letters and words.

Reading Comprehension—(50 items) measures a child's ability to comprehend what has been read. The student is required to respond orally and gesturally. For example, a problem may require the student to "pick up a ring, put it on one of his or her fingers, and rotate the ring several times." To receive credit the student must "act out" the commands.

Math Application—(60 items) measures a child's mathematical skills as they relate to real life situations.

Math Computation—(60 items) measures a child's ability to solve word problems using addition, subtraction, multiplication, and division.

Woodcock-Johnson Psychoeducational Battery—Revised (WJP-R) (Woodcock and Mather, 1989)

The WJP-R is a very popular battery that is composed of a series of subtests known as Tests of Cognitive Ability as well as a series of subtests known as Tests of Achievement.

The Tests of Cognitive Ability is broken down into seven factors:

1) **Long Term Retrieval**—measures long-term memory for both visual and auditory channels.

2) **Short Term Memory**—measures short-term memory.

3) **Processing Speed**—measures a child's ability to rapidly process visual material.

4) **Visual Processing**—measures visual problem solving skills.

5) **Comprehension Knowledge**—measures listening comprehension as well as vocabulary skills.

6) **Auditory Processing**—measures auditory problem solving skills.

7) **Fluid Reasoning**—measures abilities to form concepts, solve verbal analogies, and use spatial skills.

The Tests of Achievement is composed of four subject areas:

1) **Reading**—measures both the ability to sound out words as well as reading comprehension skills.

2) **Mathematics**—measures basic calculation skills as

well as the ability to solve real life math problems.

3) **Written Language**—measures punctuation, spelling, and actual written production of language.

4) **Knowledge**—measures factual knowledge of science, social studies, and humanities.

While the Tests of Cognitive Ability is a good measure of processing strengths and weaknesses, it should not be used as a replacement for an intelligence test such as the WISC-III or the K-ABC.

The WJP-R is an excellent instrument, but it is an extremely long test to administer. Administering both the Cognitive and Achievement section can take over two hours. Many psychologists and psychometrists simply don't have the time to use the WJP-R.

BIBLIOGRAPHY

Bard, J. and H. Fisher. "A Rational-Emotive Approach to Underachievement" in *Rational-Emotive Approaches to the Problems of Childhood*. A. Ellis and M. Bernard, editors. New York: Plenum Press, 1983.

Beck, A. and B. Shaw. "Cognitive Approaches to Depression" in *Handbook of Rational-Emotive Therapy*. A. Ellis and R. Grieger, editors. New York: Springer Press, 1977.

Clay, M. *Early Detection of Reading Difficulties*. Portsmouth, NH: Heinemann, 1986.

Felton, G. and B. Biggs. *Up from Underachievement*. Springfield, IL: Charles Thomas, 1977.

Heacox, D. *Up from Underachievement*. Minneapolis, MN: Free Spirit Publishing, 1991.

Jastak, S. and G. Wilkinson. *Manual for Wide Range Achieve-*

ment Test—revised. Wilmington, DE: Jastak Associates, 1984.

Kaufman, A. and N. Kaufman. *Manual for Kaufman Test of Educational Achievement*. Circle Pines, MN: AGS, 1985.

———. *Manual for Kaufman Assessment Battery for Children*. Circle Pines, MN: AGS, 1983.

Kelley, M. *School-Home Notes: Promoting Children's Success*. New York: Guilford Press, 1990.

Knaus, W. "Children and Low Frustration Tolerance". *Rational-Emotive Approaches to the Problems of Childhood*. A. Ellis and M. Bernard, editors. New York: Plenum Press, 1983.

McCall, R., C. Evahn. and L. Kratzer. *High School Underachievers: What Do They Achieve as Adults?* Newbury Park, CA: Sage, 1992.

Otto, L., V. Call. and K. Spenner. *Design for a Study of Entry into Careers*. Lexington, MA: Lexington, 1981.

Rimm, S. *How to Parent So Children Will Learn*. Watertown, WI: Apple Publishing, 1990.

Rotter, J., M. Seeman. and S. Liverant. "Internal Versus External Control of Reinforcement: A Major Variable in Behavior Theory". N. Washburne, editor. *Decisions, Values, and Groups*. New York: Pergamon, 1962.

Shaw, M. and McCuen, J. "The Onset of Academic Underachievement in Bright Children." *The Journal of Educational Psychology*. 51 (3) 103–108, 1960.

Weschler, D. *Manual for Weschler Intelligence Scale for Children—third edition*. San Antonio, TX: The Psychological Corporation, 1991.

———. *Manual for Weschler Preschool Primary Scale of Intelligence—revised*. San Antonio, TX: The Psychological Corporation, 1989.

———. *Manual for the Weschler Intelligence Scale for Children—revised*. New York: The Psychological Corporation, 1974.

Wilde, J. *Rational Counseling with School-Aged Popula-*

tions: A Practical Guide. Muncie, IN: Accelerated Development, 1992.

————. *The Effects of the Let's Get Rational Boardgame on Rational Thinking, Depression, and Self Acceptance in Adolescents.* Unpublished doctoral dissertation: Marquette University, 1993.

Woodcock, R. and N. Mather. *Manual for the Woodcock-Johnson Psychoeducational Battery.* Allen, TX: DLM Teaching Resources, 1989.